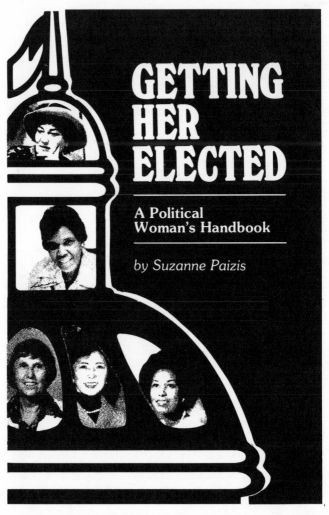

GETTING HER ELECTED

A Political Woman's Handbook

by Suzanne Paizis

Pictured on cover (top-bottom): Former U.S. Congresswoman Bella Abzug; U.S. Congresswoman Barbara Jordan; (left-right) Connecticut Governor Ella Grasso; California Secretary of State March Fong Eu; and U.S. Congresswoman Yvonne Brathwaite Burke.

GETTING HER ELECTED

ELECTED

A Political Woman's Handbook

By Suzanne Paizis

With a Foreword by
March Fong Eu

CREATIVE EDITIONS
Sacramento, California

International Standard Book Number: 0-917982-03-7
Library of Congress Catalogue Card Number: 76-29493

Printed by Spilman Printing Company, Sacramento, CA

Edited by Kathleen Campbell Anderson and Marcia McQuern

Illustrations by Melinda Frivold Iverson

Cover design by Ian McVarish

DEDICATION

To my daughters and yours . . .
Varvara, Melanie, and Kathleen . . .

Foreword

I think none of us can deny the fact that women have traditionally found greater barriers to effective campaigning than men. We're inexperienced, and often not comfortable asking people for money, for example.

Nevertheless, none of us can deny that women are entering the political field with ever-increasing success. A glance at the Certified List of Candidates for the 1976 elections revealed a tremendous number of female contenders for seats in the State Senate, Assembly, the U.S. Congress, and even for President.

I am proud of the strides we women are making in the political field, and I encourage women with serious intentions of running for office to read this well-written, well-documented, and common sense book about how to win an election.

MARCH FONG EU
California Secretary of State

Table of Contents

Introduction

A group of women and a few men came to-gether to help a political novice, who had the additional disadvantage of being a woman, run for a major state office. This attempt to elect the first woman to the California State Senate was an experience that opened many new doors for those involved. As the campaign progressed, the staff and volunteers came to realize that the experience was a novel one for women. They also began to recognize that they were developing a special expertise. It is this know-how, this expertise about running a woman's campaign that I, that woman candi-date, want to share with women who will be making similar attempts. This book is for them, in the knowledge that they will increase in number and grow in success.

If there had been a handbook such as this,

my campaign would have been off to a better start. It would have offered a foundation for organization. It would have reinforced ideas about what a woman's campaign could achieve and how to accomplish our goals.

Everyone who participated emerged with a significant increase in self-esteem. Women who worked for the first time at decision-making levels developed respect for themselves and for women as a political group. They developed a higher self expectancy, and a purposeful, realistic attitude about where women should go in politics, how they could get there and why they should be part of the action.

The men on the staff began to comprehend how prevalent sex discrimination is as they saw it manifested during the campaign. They noted the condescension, covert hostility, disdain and disregard for a woman's campaign apparent in many quarters.

Though the campaign produced few converts to radical feminism, everyone acquired a new respect for the women's movement and its role in developing women as actualized human beings with equal advantages and opportunities.

The campaign was conducted in four central California coast counties against a Republican incumbent for twenty-six years, who had faced opposition only twice in his career. Such entrenchment enabled him to retain his seat.

There was a district Democratic registration of 55.4%, but a Democratic voting record of

36%. That meant that this was not considered a priority district by the Democratic party. And that fact, plus the size and diversity of the district, gave additional advantages to the incumbent.

Hundreds of miles of choice California coastline and agriculturally productive interior valleys have produced two divergent social and political cultures. Great wealth and a resort atmosphere exist next to the poverty, frustration and anger of a large Mexican American farmworker population. Voters in the coastal communities squabbled over land usage while voters in the agricultural community measured a candidate by his/her stand on gun control.

Planning a campaign to reach the student voter meant appealing to both radical students at the University of California in Santa Cruz (where I received 91.4% of the vote), as well as to conservative ones at California Polytechnic State University in San Luis Obispo (where I received 40.6% of the student vote).

In addition to dealing with these contrasts, there were the usual issues of taxation, education, conservation and marijuana.

Essentially, the campaign was conducted for three reasons. The first was to win. The second was to articulate issues so that the incumbent would be forced to speak about them and defend his record. Just the existence of an opponent affected his performance. His support of certain legislation, his greater openness and responsiveness to the constituency were in evidence during and shortly following the campaign. The third reason was to educate the community to the fact that women can and should aspire to high political office, and to demonstrate that they can be serious, credible candidates.

There are several reasons my campaign was not successful. Beating an incumbent is always difficult, and it is almost impossible for a political novice. Also, I was a moderate liberal running in a conservative area and I was able to raise only about a quarter of the money the incumbent spent. Finally, the community had never before been asked to elect a woman for the State Senate. That was an idea that needed getting used to.

Some may say it is presumptuous to write a book about a losing campaign, just as some said it was presumptuous to attempt the campaign in the first place. It is time that women, who are 53% of the population, presume that they have a rightful place in the decision-making bodies of the states and the nation. I hope that by writing about the lessons learned in one woman's effort to achieve that place, others will get there.

Every political campaign has its own flavor and style, its own unique problems, drama and humor. Please use this book as a point from whch to deviate. Adapt the contents to your purpose.

Courage and endurance are needed for the endeavor. It is not an uphill battle, but a perpendicular one. It is a battle, too, as every real success will have to be fought for. Keep your capacity for humor readily available. It will help out in those moments of despair, frustration and embarrassment which will occur. You may have to think of all your efforts as a pioneering venture. You are really breaking new territory. We hope this handbook will give you practical assistance as well as determination and support needed for the task.

Where Women Stand

Women are the backbone of the American political structure. Since women party volunteers outnumber men ten to one, no political candidate has a chance of success without the many dedicated hours of work that women contribute to campaigns. Yet, few women are themselves candidates for office, few are hired as key staff members, and only a token number have been elected to national office.

Since 1920, when American women finally won the right to cast a ballot, the number of female voters has risen steadily to the point that today there are more women voters than men voters. And, yet, there are no women among the the one hundred United States senators. There are only 18 women, among 435 members, in the 95th Congress. There are only two women governors.

Despite the fact that more and more women have participated in the political process in recent years, very few inroads have been made when it comes to getting women elected. It is still exceedingly difficult for a woman to be elected on her own merit.

In 1974, Ella Grasso successfully campaigned in Connecticut to become the first woman governor elected on her own, and not as a successor to her husband. (Governors Nellie Taylor Ross of Wyoming, Mariam Ferguson of Texas, and Lurleen Wallace of Alabama all had husbands in office before them.)

Of the 19 women in the 94th Congress, 12 were re-elected incumbents; Marilyn Lloyd (D., Tenn.) replaced her husband; Shirley Pettis (R., Calif.) was also elected to her husband's seat (by a special election in 1975), after he was killed in a plane crash. This means that only five new women were elected to that Congress on their own. Not an overwhelming change in the status quo.

Nor did the 1976 elections demonstrate much growth in terms of women winning office. Although the number of women who ran for office increased 8.5% from 1974, the number who succeeded was minimal:

• A reduction of one Congresswoman brought the U.S. Congress' female representation in 1977 to 18 (less than 4%). Moreover, the loss of two seasoned Congresswomen, Bella Abzug (D., N.Y.) and Patsy Mink (D., Hawaii) will be noticed. Both women gave up safe House seats to run for the U.S. Senate. Both were narrowly defeated by men in the primary.

• No women were elected to the U.S. Senate.

• One new woman governor was elected in 1976. Dixie Lee Ray of Washington became the second woman in history to win a state governorship on her own.

• The 1976 elections brought an approximate 1% increase in the number of women entering state houses, bringing that total to 9.1% nationally.

The fact is, the more powerful and well-paid an elective office, the fewer number of women found in that position. Conversely, the less powerful and lower-paid the elective office is, the fewer number of men found in that position.

The state legislatures, such as New York's and California's, which are considered the most professional because they are fulltime; receive high salaries, significant benefits and retirement systems; have substantial staff allowances and paid committee consultants, have the fewest number of female legislators.

In the 1976 California race, eight women, from among 31 who appeared on the ballot as major party nominations, won seats in Congressional, state Senate or state Assembly districts — an increase of three.

California finally got its first woman senator in history when Rose Ann Vuich, a conservative Democrat, was elected in the rural San Joaquin Valley. Senator Vuich is an unmarried

3

accountant-farmer. Her race was hardly noticed in the press — while three liberal-leaning, female state Senate contenders from the Los Angeles area, who were considered likely to win, received wide attention.

Three black women from Southern California were elected or re-elected to state Assembly or Congress*, with strong support from either Los Angeles Mayor Thomas Bradley or California Lieutenant Governor Mervin Dymally. Although these three Democratic women are considered to be on the liberal side of the political spectrum, they are not necessarily oriented toward women's issues.

Three other of California's women elected to Congress or Assembly are Republicans with conservative leanings†. This means that seven of the eight women elected to high office‡ in California in 1976 appear to be conservative when it comes to support of the women's movement — in fact, some may actively disassociate themselves from it. The California example may be representative of the national picture.

The present situation is such that party leaders, always on the lookout for the most viable candidates, may be turning more and more often

4

---

*Yvonne Brathwaite Burke was re-elected to U.S. Congress; Teresa Hughes was re-elected and Maxine Waters elected to state Assembly.

†Shirley Pettis was re-elected to U.S. Congress; Carol Hallett and Marilyn Ryan were elected to state Assembly.

‡Leona Egeland, elected to her second term, has proved to be a leader in women's concerns.

to women. But the woman candidate who will be sought in the same way as the man, is likely to be a conservative Democrat or Republican without an activist background or a desire to upset the status quo. The conservative woman candidate will be able to seek funding from traditional sources, and it will be there, or it will seek her out.

Incumbent legislators, in particular, comprehend women's growing electability and the "trendiness" of supporting a woman candidate. This is an interesting disposition and can be related to the fact that male legislators sense the presence of a powerful women's constituency, which they make a point of being sensitive to.

Those women being elected today are not running on feminist platforms. Women's organizations, as yet, lack the unity and political clout to elect their own candidates. The women who have worked the hardest to open the political arena to other women, may be the last to personally benefit from this new attitude.

5

In the future power-makers will be looking for women candidates, visible women who reflect the standards of the community. The next step is for women to run who have the political acuity to appear safe to the party structure and who have the courage to be innovative once elected.

It is still too early to speculate on how women will perform in the higher arenas of political power. Changing the priorities advocated and protected by male-dominated institutions must be viewed as a major, if not radical, undertaking.

And if women, once elected, are not willing to undertake that task, then why bother electing women? What we can work toward are growing numbers of elected women who will maintain their own style and not be co-opted into the male politics-as-usual world. It will take women of exceptional ability, vision and determination to bring a new quality into the political process.

This is the great political challenge for women who are willing to make the attempt. It is also a challenge for all those people who help such women get elected. Without them, she has no chance for success. And when the campaign hoopla is over, they are the experienced people who continue to live in communities, supporting and molding an equitable and open political process — a process that should guarantee the very best individuals will become candidates, and that they will have an opportunity to be elected.

6

The Special Difficulties

There are a number of factors which effect political success. Most of them work against women.

The two most important factors in winning an election are being an incumbent and outspending your opponent. About 90% of incumbents running for re-election win. And, incumbents usually are able to raise and spend two to five times the amount of money that challengers can raise and spend. This puts female candidates in something of a "Catch 22" situation. They are not incumbents so they do not have the money-raising ability of incumbents to gain office to become incumbents.

Another important factor in winning is the name recognition of the candidate. Incumbents already have name identification in the community, an advantage their widows inherit. Usually,

7

male challengers have some degree of name recognition in the business, professional, or political community, so can raise money from these sources to get their names better known.

For example, the success of actor Ronald Reagan in his first political campaign for governor of California was based, in large part, on the fact that he was already known to millions of people through his movie and TV career.

Most women simply do not have these political success prerequisites. A study of the media representation of women showed that they were mentioned in newspapers, radio or TV less than 30% of the time. And about 80% of those mentions were of Patty Hearst or Lynnette "Squeaky" Fromme, the Manson family member who tried to shoot President Ford. The other 20% were the wives and daughters of current or former presidents, movie stars and victims of crimes. Very few women acquire the kind of name recognition which will give a boost to a political career. If they do something it is usually reported on the women's page.

A further disadvantage for the female would-be candidate is how she becomes a candidate. Women are outside the process whereby business, professional, or party machinery selects, encourages and primes one of its own to run for office. Women therefore do not have the same avenues of access to money and influence as men do. They have been excluded from decision-making levels, they don't play golf or tennis with "fat cats," they don't casually drop

8

into the bar or restaurant for social and political contacts, and they never are members of the respected "male clubs" which are frequently the first rungs on the political ladder.

More often, women seek office after years of community volunteer work. Billions of dollars of volunteer work have been contributed by community women to education, health services, politics, religious and charitable organizations. If women stopped giving away their time and talent, the way society functions would alter radically. Yet this volunteer effort on the part of women has not been recognized in gross national product figures, or on a woman's own work experience record. Women have to work much harder to prove their capabilities, they are forced into circuitous routes for success, and they must constantly compensate for the inclination men have to overlook or underrate them.

In effect, women are playing the game in another ballpark than men with a different set of rules. Under those conditions, it is hard for a woman to be a member of the political team.

These are the odds that a woman candidate will encounter. Some of the special problems will be discussed in more detail later. Generally, women will find it difficult to be taken seriously as candidates. Society is still reluctant to accept women in leadership positions.

There is a brighter side to the story of women in politics, however. On the local level, women are beginning to run and win elections in greater numbers. National figures show that 10% of school trustees are women and 19% of city council members are women. (In California, 23% of school trustees are women.)

There are two sobering points to consider when we look at the growing number of women elected to local office. First, the public management system has grown considerably in the last two decades, diminishing the decision-making powers of locally elected officials. School superintendents and city or county administrators are the power centers. Boards and councils, where women sit, make only general policy and serve as a community sounding board.

Secondly, the taxing and legislating powers of local jurisdictions have been seriously eroded by state and national laws. The dollars-and-cents political power once held by school trustees and council members no longer exists. Because of this lessening of power, influential men in the community no longer compete for these seats. The field is more open to women candidates.

These facts in no way diminish the contributions of women elected officials at the local level. Women *should* actively seek these seats. Their participation provides significant service to the community and should be encouraged. Moreover, it is vitally important for women to serve as role models for other women. What better way than to see women involved at the local level?

Perhaps for women, as for men, winning a local campaign may be the steppingstone to higher office. Women's aspirations are rising in

10

all fields. There are places where women are still ridiculed for aspiring to anything more than home and hearth. Yet, options and opportunities are opening to women in fields previously closed to them. Many women now see that a career and family are not mutually exclusive for them any more than a career and family are mutually exclusive for a man. Many more women are eager to participate in government.

As more and more women become politically prominent in their communities, other women will identify with them. They will be more accepted as leaders by both men and women. Little girls can grow up wanting to be President just like little boys do. And one day, one of them *will* be President.

11

12

Qualifications

Recent figures show that women who run for political office are better educated than their male counterparts. Many of them are married and can spend more time than men at jobs which compensate only for expenses.

Women are perceived as more honest, less likely to be "on the take" than their male peers, mostly because they are not involved in the business world. They are thought to be less defensive and ego-involved and more willing to question or admit they don't know something.

Women do their homework more consistently than their fellow board or council members and are more likely to have studied issues at hand. Again, that may be a case of having time, since many of them are not the main support of families. Women who must support themselves

13

and their families are less likely to be involved at this level of politics.

These factors, plus other qualities women possess, may be future assets in the political structure. Women may have different priorities than men, and they may hold different attitudes about problems and solutions. They may, as women, be more accessible to groups which, at present, have little or no access to the political process. The ties and communication systems they have in the community are different than those men have. They may be able to bring a wider scope of people and ideas into the system. Their fresh approach and different perspective may make the process more responsive to human needs.

14

Politicians come in assorted packages: large, small, young, old, rich, poor. However, there are some general attributes a viable candidate should have. They are:

A background that will bear public scrutiny.

Once a candidate, one is a public person. Voters will be interested in the candidate's family and personal history. Her private life may become a campaign issue, a possibility which should be considered before a decision to run is made.

An open attitude and an easiness with people.

Meeting, speaking with and listening to people will be the daily job for candidate and elected official. There will be new experiences, contacts with different kinds of people. The candidate's ability to take new experiences in stride and to communicate with all kinds of people in a friendly, concerned fashion is important.

Demonstrated competence in professional, business, community or political fields.

The old saying that a woman has to be twice as good as a man to be successful is twice as important in politics. Perhaps that means a woman candidate has to be four times better. Many men who seek to enter politics plan a participation and achievement campaign for many years before they finally enter the right race at the right time. They join groups, work on community projects, participate in political party activities, become noteworthy in their field or profession and do good things for special groups. Women must also design and implement the same kind of personal plan in preparation for political candidacy.

15

Ability to articulate ideas and to feel comfortable in a variety of speaking situations.

During the course of the campaign the candidate will have opportunities to speak with small informal groups and large formal groups. She will have to address friendly audiences, hostile audiences, convince doubters, and present her platform clearly. This will occur at various times: under the pressure of a three-minute speech, a thirty-second radio spot, or a forty-minute presentation.

High concentration and energy.

Being a candidate for office demands a person spend long hours at the job, not get discouraged easily, and make decisions under pressure while in public view. A candidate has to get into the campaign all the way. She can't make it if half-hearted about the endeavor.

Outlook which can accept personal criticism or lack of support.

Campaigns can end old friendships and build lasting new ones. Both support and opposition will come from surprising places. The reasons why people do or do not support a candidate can be an enigma. Their support can come because they like the platform or because they hate the opponent. They may work for the candidate because she is the first real live candidate they have met, or work against her because they don't believe she is qualified. The candidate must accept the support graciously and discount the lack of it without rancor.

Reputation for integrity and ability to do a job.

It is a tremendous asset for the campaign if people think of the candidate as an honest, reliable person who can get the job done. That kind of reputation takes time to build, and the candidate has to be the kind of person to get the image across.

16

Finance

For a candidate, money should be neither a bar nor an entry into public office. As much as many of us would like to believe that statement, money will be of major concern to anyone running for public office. Especially, if that person is a woman — unless she is independently wealthy.

17

Most of us would like to think that our elected officials have not been influenced by the size of a campaign check. However, when state campaigns can cost as much as a quarter of a million dollars, it is naive to believe that money does not buy future votes.

Campaign finance reform laws have been passed in recent years with the intention of restoring competition to the process by giving challengers a better chance to run effective campaigns. Those laws seek to (1) reduce the effect special interests have over the election process by limiting the amount they give to candidates; (2) require candidate disclosure of money sources; (3) require candidate (and elected official) disclosure of investment and real property interests; and (4) limit campaign expenditures.

In many states candidates for federal office must file copies of their federal statements with appropriate state officials. All candidates for federal, state, and local office should check with the County Board of Elections for details of finance laws governing campaigns. Forms and manuals may be obtained locally or from the (state) Secretary of State's office.

Because the new laws require a careful accounting of all contributions and expenditures, be prepared to have both legal and accounting assistance throughout the campaign. The statements required are complex and constantly changing, and many a candidate's ignorance has resulted in a news story about his/her failure to comply with finance laws.

Fairly early, most women will realize that they are not able to raise the same amounts of money as their male counterparts, nor acquire it from the same sources. Money will be much harder to get.

There are a number of ways in which early money can be obtained. The first, and perhaps most important way for a number of reasons, is for the candidate to meet with those people in and out of the community who are regular and large contributors to party candidates. She and the Finance Coordinator should have a personal meeting with each one who is uncommitted to a competitor.

This may be an individual or a small group meeting, but known party contributors should have the opportunity to assess the candidate. They should hear about her campaign strategy, her stands on issues, and have the opportunity to observe her personal style in listening and talking to potential constituents.

The one area in the finance picture which the candidate does *not* delegate to other staff members is asking for contributions from legislators, state leaders and other major contributors. The candidate herself needs to deal directly with these people as it will be much more difficult to give her a "no" than to turn down a staff member.

19

The candidate should also plan on meeting with wealthy or influential women in the community who are not usually approached through regular political channels. They may be very responsive to the candidacy of a woman due to shared concerns over particular social issues such as health care, child care, etc.

Other fund-raising beginnings may occur with the usual kinds of events (lunches, dinners, cocktail parties, celebrity receptions, bake sales, bazaars, rummages, etc.). These will introduce a large number of workers into the campaign and get the candidate's name known in the area, as well as build up a bank account.

Another method is to start an early mailing

solicitation to friends, acquaintances, party members, and other potential supporters. Small amounts of money, pledged over a period of a year (from one November to the next) are not a hardship to persons who are excited about a candidate. Fifty or more persons pledging from $5 to $100 per month for that year will enable the campaign to meet basic staff and operating needs. This kind of basic support will not only create a strong financial base for the campaign, it will also do a great deal for the morale of the entire campaign staff.

You will need to use a combination of the above strategies. First, party regulars are going to continue to be important in the success of your efforts. If you cannot enlist their financial support at first, you can attempt to neutralize them until the field of candidates is known. When your candidate becomes the party nominee you will continue to need support, enthusiasm and contributions from people who have a great deal of influence and wide-ranging contacts within the community.

Secondly, when people give or help raise money for the campaign, they make a commitment to your candidacy. Those people who cannot give money, but who give their time and effort to help are as important to the campaign for the same reasons.

Finally, because different sources tend to dry up during the campaign year, you will need versatility to develop expertise in the ways of raising money. The earlier you and the staff begin, the more methods and contacts you make, the better you will become at the task and the sooner you will have money to work with.

Money raised early in the primary or in June and July of the regular campaign is "worth more" than money raised in November. Why? Because it allows the Campaign Manager to do many things that will not be possible later in the fall. For example, early money will allow purchase of television time, radio spots and newspaper space which will be at a premium later in the fall. It will guarantee the best time and the best spot. It will also make direct mail plans a reality. Letters mailed too close to election day will probably arrive at their destination after the election, as post offices are inundated with political material. Campaign literature, bumper stickers, pins, balloons and so forth which are important in getting the candidate's name around should be distributed early in August and September. Coordination, planning, printing and distribution all take time. Early money gives early planning the boost it needs.

21

Remember, too that there is *no credit* for the non-incumbent candidate for public office. The standard is cash on the line, paid in full in advance, or as in the case of telephones, a hefty deposit for each phone for every month. Everyone — state, national, local candidates and all of the ballot proponent groups — will be competing for similar things simultaneously. Prime time. Prime attention. Prime money.

Once a candidate files for office and the

campaign is underway, financing of the campaign should become independent of the candidate. Raising money is an anxiety-provoking, detailed and frustrating chore. The candidate should be spared such details and frustrations which will and do occur in every campaign. She should not have to feel personally obligated to everyone who contributes to her campaign, nor should she have to be exposed to the disappointing elements of fund-raising. Finally, she does not have to know the dollar amounts that friends and acquaintances have or have not contributed.

This is *not* to say that the candidate should not know what is going on in her campaign. She should know who the large contributors are, what organizations will or will not support her and why. The processes for getting endorsements (money) from labor unions, professional organizations and other lobbying interests all become strategies which must include her. She must be informed and make decisions about accepting all large contributions. However, she does not need to experience nitty-gritty details or disappointments.

It is probably going to be necessary for a woman candidate to do some "educating" in the attitude of society toward contributing money to women and in amounts they are accustomed to giving. While "she" is writing a $5 check for her favorite woman candidate (and considering that a sizeable donation), "he" is writing a $50 or a

22

$500 check for the candidate of his choice (usually male).

Most women have not considered themselves responsible for the financial support of the political process. They have allowed this particular aspect to be men's responsibility. Good government, which means those elected officials who make the idea of good government a reality, must be supported by *all* of the citizens, not only by the male citizens, in order to encourage the full participation of all people. A woman candidate must be something of a teacher, which is not the usual role of a politician. She may have to educate other women and men to become substantial supporters of women candidates.

Part of the reason women are not taken seriously as candidates for high political office is that the qualities of leadership are thought of as male qualities. Most voters are accustomed to male leadership, whether, in fact, such leadership does or does not exist in a given individual male. A reconditioning process is needed for society to think of women as having the dynamic qualities which make for leadership.

Part of a woman's credibility as a leader will, paradoxically, depend upon the amount of money she will be able to raise during the campaign. Yet, because she is a woman, she will not be able to raise the same amount of money as her male counterpart. Instead, she will have to rely on smaller amounts from greater numbers of people, she will have to rely on greater efforts from smaller numbers of people, and this will

23

take more time, greater talent and endurance from everyone concerned.

Another consideration for the woman candidate is the spending philosophy of the campaign. The personal resources of the candidate, and how willing she is to go into debt, are critical factors. If married with a young family and not independently wealthy, she will have to consider the degree to which she and her husband may carry a financial burden once the campaign is over.

For most women's campaigns, a moderate pay-as-you-go plan should be followed. This is a sound policy as it will indicate her philosophical attitude toward spending if she is elected.

24

Finally, an extremely important part of a woman's campaign is to get the women who participate in the campaign to think of themselves as "fund-raisers" or "finance chairpersons." Most of the small dollar amounts raised in any organization are raised through the efforts of women, but it is not often that a woman heads the money committee. Most women who take on money-raising jobs can be as successful at the task as men if they develop a consciousness that they can raise money and that it is their responsibility. The ingredients for success are commitment to the candidate, a sense of personal ability for the task, and some solid techniques.

FINANCE COORDINATOR

The role of the Finance Coordinator is of key importance in the campaign. Usually, it is a man of wealth and respect in the community who uses his personal wealth, persuasion and prestige to raise money privately. In a woman's campaign, it may be more difficult to recruit someone of this stature, depending upon the woman and the race. It may be that the woman candidate will rely on the wife of this kind of man or on women who are wealthy in their own right.

The duties of the Finance Coordinator are to:

1. Contribute substantially to the campaign. The individual who can and will do so, will have much more clout with other potential donors.

2. Serve as a member of the Executive Staff working under the direction of the Campaign Manager.

25

3. Recruit Finance Committee members: Treasurer, Fund-Raising Chair, Events Chair.

4. Perhaps serve as a member of the Budget Committee.

5. With the Campaign Manager, determine the master plan for raising money for the campaign.

6. Recruit others to assist in personal solicitations, and to give major fund-raising events.

7. Carry out all finance and fund-raising plans in accordance with Budget Committee and Executive Staff decisions.

FUND-RAISING CHAIR

The second most important position in the financial hierarchy is that of the Fund-Raising Chair. Money which is solicited on a private and personal level, we term "finance raising" and money which is acquired through events we term "fund-raising." As the processes are different and the people needed for each activity are different, we establish two separate committees. Those individuals who have the status to raise money privately are not the people who will be interested in handling the activities of smaller events. Fund-raising events derive money from items for sale or from admissions or from both. Numbers of people are needed to carry out the details of the activity.

26

The duties of the Fund-Raising Chair are to:

1. Serve as a member of the Finance Committee.

2. Perhaps serve on the Budget Committee, but definitely provide input into committee processes.

3. Recruit Events Chairpersons who will sponsor money-raising activities.

4. Call and preside at planning meetings for large fund-raising activities.

5. Organize all fund-raising activities including sales events, barbecues, picnics, wine-tastings, auctions, dances, testimonial dinners, etc.

6. Keep list of individuals who work on fund-raising events and see that they are thanked through Headquarters Manager.

TREASURER

The Campaign Treasurer is the third component of the money triumvirate. Generally, the Treasurer is the person who handles all of the money.

The duties of the Treasurer are to:

1. Serve as a member of the Budget Committee.

2. Open a bank account.

3. Sign all checks as Treasurer. (Consider having multiple signatures for expenditure approval. Co-signers may be the Finance Chair, Headquarters Manager, Campaign Manager.)

27

4. Receive all contributions, receipts, bills, etc.

5. Keep an account of moneys received, dispersed, accounts paid. Set up bookkeeping systems in branch offices.

6. Fill out campaign expense forms required by law.

7. Keep Campaign Manager and Executive Staff informed through regular reports of financial aspects of the campaign and of campaign finance law.

FUND-RAISING EVENTS CHAIR

Fund-raising events come in many forms. They range from small neighborhood events to expensive $1,000 a plate dinners. Small fund-raisers bring in one or two hundred dollars and may consist of a luncheon, bridge party or simple supper where a small contribution is requested. Neighborhood barbecues, progressive dinners or picnics are good ways of getting people together to become acquainted with the campaign and of obtaining a small amount of money. The candidate may or may not be present at such an event.

The kinds of fund-raisers which normally bring in amounts from $200 to $1,000 include auctions, rummage and garage sales, carnivals or international bazaars with ethnic goods and foods. At the very top of fund-raising events are the expensive testimonial dinners which are legion with politicians (and dull). There are easily available a number of well written books dealing with fund-raising ideas. We are more interested in giving you an idea about the management of such events. It will be necessary for you to adapt the fund-raising ideas to your campaign and your area.

In close cooperation with the Fund-Raising Chair, *the duties of the Events Chair are to:*

Recruit a committee and with the committee, plan each event in detail.

Members of the Committee will need to:

1. Issue invitations or make announce-

ments of events (written, telephone, newspaper, paid advertising, etc.).

2. Make telephone follow-up calls.

3. Determine refreshments and volunteers to donate, serve, clean up, etc.

4. Determine other items, articles, services needed, when and how.

5. Arrange places for events.

6. Through Fund-Raising Chair, keep staff in touch with plans, distribute press releases and coordinate candidate's schedule.

7. Be present at activities.

8. Keep lists of all persons who donate time, money or service to the events so they can be thanked.

29

9. See that the Fund-Raising Chair receives lists of contributions and contributors.

10. Serve as contact persons for the candidate and her Aide.

BUDGET

As early as possible a tentative budget must be set up by the Campaign Manager and the Treasurer. It should set the dollar goal which is based upon amounts spent in previous elections and should anticipate what the opponent will be spending this election. It must build a money *raising* time line which will anticipate the money *spending* time line.

Members of the Executive Staff should submit to the Finance Committee itemized budgets for their committee operations. These must include the anticipated expenditures and the time at which those expenditures will be made.

Two alternative budgets should be set up. One, an actual budget which you will work to realize, and the other a minimum budget with a priority needs list. You will then know how much money will be needed at a given time to do a job properly. Staff decisions to cut or trim budget items will be based on priority needs rather than on hasty decisions.

The best way to work out the budget is to start from election day and work backwards day by day for the last two weeks of the campaign, and then week by week. The *needs schedule* and the *fund-raising schedule* may be adjusted to anticipate heavy spending periods. These flow charts help make scheduling decisions for fund-raising, solicitation mailings, or telephone drives. (See proposed *Budget Flow Chart.*)

Clear guidelines and areas of budget responsibility should be set up early for smooth and efficient operations. Staff must be informed of the process for spending authorization, changing major budgeted items in crisis situations, and of their responsibilities for staying within the budget. Staff members should be expected to obtain bids or estimates for major jobs. Some type of requisitioning procedure needs to be set up by the Finance Committee. The techniques of ordering and distribution will be similar to

30

those in business, but accomplished in less time because of the swift-moving quality of a political campaign.

A dollar goal should be set for each identifiable community based on population and income levels. If people give money to a candidate, they usually cast a vote for that candidate. Therefore you want to get as large a contribution from as many people as possible.

We found that individual donors were frequently more willing to contribute money to a specific item than to the general campaign fund. During fund-raising operations a pitch was made to pay for a particular project: $185 for bumper stickers, $39 for office stationery, $425 for a newspaper ad. The pitch was geared to the size and affluence of the group to which it was made. This gave people a better idea of campaign spending amounts and priorities, and it made them feel more personally involved by knowing where their money was going to be spent. Somehow, they don't like to think they are paying for staff. There is a tendency to feel that most work for a political campaign should be volunteered. Most contributors prefer to pay for things rather than for people.

Campaign money always should be spent where it will do the most good. As often as possible, doing business with local firms is best. In rural communities, it may be cheaper to send your business to a large urban area, but those few extra dollars spent at a local business may well return extra votes. Also, money raised in one community for newspaper or radio ads should, when possible, be spent at the newspaper or radio station serving that area. Your contributors will want evidence that you are spending where you said you would spend.

On the next page is a breakdown of expenditures in one campaign.

Telephone expenses were high (8.5%) because the district covered four counties, and interoffice communication concerning scheduling, candidate appearances, materials, etc. was frequent.

32

The media survey demonstrated that radio was the dominant vehicle since 18 radio stations served different communities. It was estimated that more people would be reached in this manner than any other, so 13% of the budget was spent on this item.

A direct mail campaign introducing the candidate and sampling the willingness of women of all political parties to vote for the candidate was conducted in September. Both contributors and campaign workers were recruited from those who returned questionnaires. Cost was about 10.5% of the total budget.

BREAKDOWN OF EXPENDITURES IN ONE CAMPAIGN

FIXED

Fees	.5%
Rental	5.5
Staff salary	16.0
	22.0%

OTHER

Office Supplies		1.5%
Photography, Graphics		1.5
Candidate Travel		2.0
Other Travel		3.0
Research		13.5
(Primary poll	4.0%)	
(Direct mail	7.5)	
(Consultant	2.0)	
Media Advertising		30.5%
(Radio	13.0)	
(Newspaper	5.5)	
(TV	12.0)	
Media Materials		7.5%
Brochures, etc.		
Telephone		8.5
Mailing		6.0
Miscellaneous		1.0
Contingency		3.0
		78.0%

33

BUDGET FLOW CHART

PROPOSED BUDGET F

Expenses	TOTAL Amount	Months before campaign:					Oct. 25
		June	July	Aug.	Sept.	Oct.	

Staff:
  Professional
  Clerical							

Office Rental:							
Office Supplies:							
Telephone:							
Photography: Graphics							

Travel:
  Candidate
  Other staff							

Research:
  Primary poll
  Direct mail survey
  Consultant fees							

Media Advertising:
  Radio
  Newspaper
  Television
  Films							

Materials:
  Brochure
  Issues papers
  Balloons
  Pins, buttons
  Lawn signs							

Mailing:
  Mailing permit fees
  Postage							

Miscellaneous:							
Contingency:							

34

	Last two weeks:									
	29	30	31	Nov. 1	2	3	4	5	6	7

35

36

Campaign Headquarters

The nature of the district in which a campaign is conducted will determine the number and location of the headquarters or offices. A candidate whose district lies in part of a large urban area will have different office and headquarters needs than a candidate whose district lies in more than one county.

Because both money and time will be spent on headquarters, the staff should determine the following before the campaign commences:

What are the specific needs for a headquarters or office?

What purposes will they serve?

What opportunities exist for cooperation with party headquarters?

What equipment and supplies will be necessary?

37

Campaign office requirements will be different before the primary than after the nomination has been won. Political parties do not endorse or financially support one candidate over another before the primary. If your party has a headquarters you will be able to display materials along with all the other party candidates for the same office. Circumstances will determine whether you need your own headquarters during the primary. Once you become the nominee and are part of the party slate, party support and endorsement are possible.

Office space may be defined as the center of a campaign organization network where staff plans strategy and works in some degree of order, privacy and quiet. Office space is where confidential files, financial records, research and strategy reports are housed. It is the nucleus whence the day-to-day flow of events, orders, messages and press reports come.

Campaign headquarters are usually found in or very close to urban centers where volunteers congregate and off-street traffic is encouraged to drop in. Candidate material such as posters, bumper stickers, pins, literature and position papers are displayed and available. Volunteer forces gather to work, and precinct and canvassing drives emanate from headquarters. Both the headquarters and office may be housed at the same location, but their functions are different. Branch locations may be set up in outlying cities and counties.

38

Other headquarters uses are:

General candidate and campaign image projection.

Storage and distribution point of materials.

Direct mail activities.

General clerical activities including typing of cards, letters, thank-you notes; duplicating and collating of material.

Telephone reception and telephone committee phone center.

What opportunities exist for participation with party headquarters?

If your party has headquarters in different communities within the district you should be able to place your material in such centers. You must be willing to allow your volunteers to help in staffing party headquarters. The purpose of this is to establish a cooperative attitude, to keep in touch with party activities and strategies, and to have your people see that your materials are in adequate supply, attractively displayed and distributed on an equal basis. There are many things which can be done with the party organization and with other candidates' workers as well. These include precinct canvassing, literature distribution, transportation and voter registration. Staff and volunteer participation will help accomplish the tasks and will effect party unity. Money and volunteer efforts should not be wasted by duplication. If you participate in party headquarters operations following the primary, you may need a smaller, less expensive office.

What equipment and supplies will be necessary?

Telephones. The campaign cannot survive without telephones. There is *no credit* with the phone company for the non-incumbent candidate. The telephone company demands a substantial minimum deposit on each phone for every month of the campaign in advance. You will need at least two telephones in every office at first. One should be kept clear for incoming calls. Arrangements with the telephone company should be made well in advance as the phone numbers should be placed on all printed materials. You will also want to be included in the **40** directory. Because the phone bill is a major budget item and can mount rapidly, the phones should be monitored by a dependable person. The number, duration and destination of all long-distance calls must be recorded.

Permanent mailing or post office addresses. These, too, will appear on all printed materials.

Branch banking facilities.

Bulk mailing permits and post office accessibility.

Office equipment: desk, typewriter, duplicating machine. If you do not have free and easy access to a mimeograph, ditto or copier, one may be rented from a local business equipment office. They are rentable on a monthly basis, and over a period of three or more months, it is cheaper and more efficient to rent a machine than to use the fast print businesses.

Stationery, envelopes, post card and other correspondence materials should be designed by the same person who designs other campaign materials. Coordination of style, print and color is important.

Storage for materials. The headquarters should be kept as tidy as possible. There is always a great deal of coming and going in campaign headquarters, but dirty coffee cups and cigarette butts do not enhance the campaign image. Needed items must be accessible, and systems for keeping records must be set up and maintained.

Volunteers, telephone callers, and drop-ins should always be met with courtesy and friendliness. Those volunteers and drop-ins are your voters and vote-getters; the headquarters staff should reflect the candidate's desired image.

41

Organizational Chart

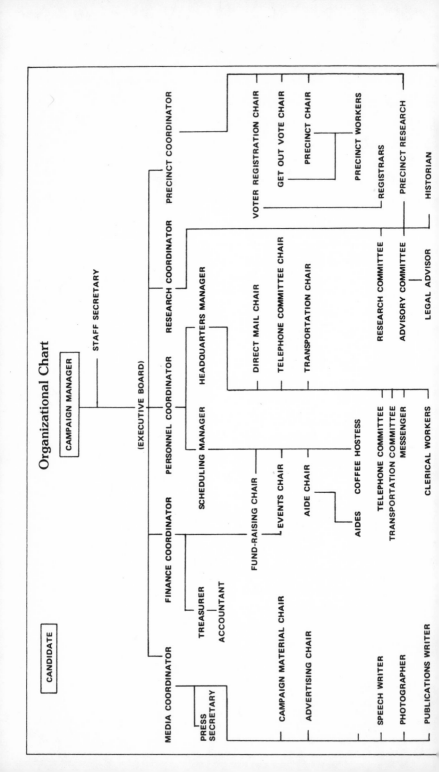

Personnel

People *are* a political campaign. From voter to volunteer to staff to candidate, politics is *people*. How effective you are in getting people to work for your campaign and to vote for the candidate is what it is all about.

43

To most voters, the only personal contact they have with a political campaign is through the young volunteer who knocks at the door or the older woman who is willing to make fifty personal telephone calls a day for the candidate. Voters will measure your entire campaign by the people they see represent you. If your workers are informed and friendly that is an asset to a campaign. If they are rude, argumentative or pushy they can only hurt your chances of success. Therefore, you must select your key campaign staff with care.

Next to raising money, one of the most difficult aspects of a campaign is what to do with volunteers. Finding meaningful, useful and necessary jobs for volunteers is quite a sensitive task. If people offer to help and are never asked, they feel hurt and left out. A talented person may be put into a dull job and leave the campaign from boredom. Or an overbearing, insensitive person may be given a key spot and literally drive people away.

A lot of people want to help, but they say they don't want to walk precincts, telephone, ask for money, type or make coffee. Often they can't or don't want to do what you need. So, it is up to your personnel staff to make all of these tasks seem easy, fun and rewarding. How this is done will be reflected in the overall quality of the campaign.

44

Since it seemed appropriate to put job descriptions in the chapters where the jobs themselves are discussed, this chapter does not include all personnel. Please refer to the Organizational Chart and chapters for Campaign Manager, Accountant, Treasurer, Legal Advisor, as well for personnel in media, research and precinct organization.

PERSONNEL COORDINATOR

The jobs of both the Scheduling Coordinator and the Headquarters Manager are responsible and time consuming. More than one county, or a number of independent cities or neighborhoods within a district, warrant more than one Scheduling Coordinator and/or Headquarters Manager.

If that is the case, a *Personnel Coordinator* who becomes a member of the Executive Staff should be selected to coordinate and direct all of those activities. If it is not necessary to select a Personnel Coordinator, then the Scheduling Coordinator and/or the Headquarters Manager should be part of the Executive Staff. Duties as described will be taken over by one or the other.

The duties of the Personnel Coordinator are to:

1. Serve as a member of the Executive Staff working under the direction of the Campaign Manager.

2. Recruit and supervise Scheduling Coordinators and Headquarters Managers.

3. Plan and direct all scheduling operations.

45

4. Plan and direct all headquarters management operations. Assist in the planning of training sessions for workers.

5. Coordinate activities between the Scheduling Coordinators and the Headquarters Managers.

6. Supervise office maintenance operations, messenger service and Speakers Bureau services.

HEADQUARTERS MANAGER

If the campaign is large enough to have more than one campaign headquarters or office locations, Headquarters Managers may be selected to work under the direction of the Personnel Coordinator.

The duties of the Headquarters Managers are to:

1. Plan and direct all headquarters management operations.

2. Recruit, direct and supervise all office and custodial workers, whether paid or unpaid.

3. Assist in training sessions for workers.

4. In coordination with the Finance Coordinator, set up the headquarters plan for receiving and dispersing money.

5. Maintain headquarters accounts and records.

6. Work closely with Precinct Coordinator and Scheduling Chair in coordinating activities.

46

SCHEDULING CHAIR

The position of the Scheduling Chair is a crucial one in the structure of the campaign. This is the person who schedules *all* of the candidate's engagements and makes decisions regarding strategy and coordination for the smooth scheduling of the candidate's time. The Chairperson should have a wide knowledge of the district and many contacts within it.

The duties of the Scheduling Chair are:

1. Keep a calendar of all appointments for the candidate.

2. Recruit persons to hold coffees, fundraisers, cocktail parties or other events.

3. Research and list all of the following in-

formation about every event the candidate will attend:

Time for arrival and departure. The candidate should arrive approximately 15 minutes after announced beginning so that guests have a chance to congregate, and depart about 15 minutes before announced ending. If the event is a business-type luncheon, be on time.

Place: address, directions (include map, telephone number).

Contact person: host, chairperson, etc. (name and status).

Time and length for candidate to speak.

Type of function: numbers in attendance, interests and emphasis of group.

Local color information for candidate's speech.

If the event is a formal "candidate's night," *information about ground rules, order of speakers, length of time for presentation and questions, etc.*

4. Make decisions on what events — such as barbecues, picnics, rallies, luncheons, parades, civic functions, testimonial dinners, park openings, dedication ceremonies — are most advantageous for the candidate to attend. Make appropriate excuses when invitations are rejected.

5. Recruit surrogate speakers for events that the candidate will not be able to attend.

47

Schedule appointments, select an Aide for the surrogate speakers.

6. Serve as liaison with party candidates and party headquarters for all the political activities which the candidate will participate in.

7. Know when party officials and candidates for other offices (e.g. President, Senator) will be making appearances in the district. Make arrangements for them to appear on the candidate's behalf, or to have the candidate appear with them at special events.

8. Offer cooperation on all party activities.

9. Work closely with Aides Chair in recruiting and training Aides.

10. Keep cool when important events which have been negotiated for months are cancelled at the last minute. Make all necessary calls the cancellation requires.

11. Maintain a backup list of other engagements for last minute cancellations so the candidate will not have an unplanned day.

It is expected that the candidate will be a person of great energy and will be appearing at many events during each day. She should be exposed to large numbers and a variety of people. Her presence (time) at such events should have a *pay off.*

Some aspects of a pay off are:

1. Press (newspaper, radio, TV) before or after the event, or a press conference or interview at the event.

2. Opportunity to be introduced to the group and to speak about her candidacy and her stand on issues.

3. Be introduced to the group by a member of the group who knows the membership and has their respect.

4. If she is not to be publicly introduced, an opportunity to meet many people quickly.

5. An opportunity to pass out literature or other material.

6. An opportunity to meet numbers of persons not easily met, such as crowds at the theaters, factories, public events, etc.

These criteria will help make decisions about which event should be selected, if there is a choice. They may also serve as a guide to getting the most out of an appearance. As an example, if the candidate plans to attend a function, but will not get press notices, nor be introduced to the group, nor have her material distributed, she would do better to spend her time elsewhere. On the other hand, it is worth going out of the way for a good interview, or to speak before a group she has had no opportunity to meet before.

49

THE AIDE

The Aide is a person who accompanies the candidate on her daily rounds of activities.

The job of Aide is probably the most interesting of all campaign jobs. It offers the stimulation of contact with people, travel and the excitement of being on the firing line with the candidate. A good Aide is a major asset to the candidate; an Aide who doesn't have a clear idea of what he/she is doing or why he/she is doing it is best left at home.

The duties of the Aide are to:

1. Attend workshop session and follow-up meetings of Aide Committee.

2. On assigned day, check with Aide Chair for packet and all pertinent information about the day's events.

3. Pick up and deliver the candidate at scheduled places.

50

4. Find contact person and introduce candidate. Make certain that contact person or another member of the group introduces the candidate to as many people as possible.

5. Confirm with chairperson the specific time the candidate will speak, length of time, determine the question and answer period, and check where candidate will speak. Test public address systems.

6. If a fund-raising pitch is to be made, determine who will make that pitch. If no one present will do it, then it will fall to the Aide. People are always more willing to give money when a member of their own group, and one with some status, asks.

7. Hand out appropriate literature, other materials.

8. Collect names and addresses of all in attendance whenever possible. Gather endorsements, names and addresses of contributors.

9. Solicit future chairpersons for coffees, luncheons, fund-raisers, etc. Solicit workers by giving short talk on where volunteers are needed, in what jobs.

10. Listen to the candidate's presentation critically. Observe, if possible, the reaction of the audience. Prepare to discuss with the candidate pertinent comments on the way to the next event.

11. Be prepared to ask a question to change the trend of the discussion if necessary and appropriate.

51

12. Help get the candidate away at the appointed time. Be careful not to interrupt the candidate if she is making an important contact, but make excuses for her when individuals involve her in long or personal conversation.

13. Thank the host as you leave. Discover the names and addresses of others who contributed significantly to the event. If you don't remember to thank them, they will remember that you didn't.

14. Keep in contact with headquarters during the day for changes in scheduling, etc.

15. After returning the candidate, complete and turn in reports and lists.

The general qualities an Aide should have are:

1. Outgoing, friendly, enjoys meeting people.

2. Knowledge of the community, community interests.

3. Good driver.

4. Ability to work with reporters, hosts, argumentative persons, etc.

Depending upon the size of the campaign, you may need from six to twelve persons to serve as Aides. Ideally, the list of men and women who will serve as Aides should include a variety of ages and interests. This gives further demonstration of the candidate's breadth of appeal. Because the Aide will be seen with and act on behalf of the candidate in a variety of situations, he/she should be selected with serious consideration of special talents and abilities.

Once the Aides are recruited, a series of training sessions should be held. As the campaign progresses, there should be periodic meetings at which Aides share experiences and refine techniques. Aides should always be kept informed of sensitive local issues when traveling with the candidate. Often they will be called upon to deal with such problems so the candidate does not have to. Some considerations in selecting the right Aide for a particular assignment are:

Who would feel most comfortable introduc-

ing the candidate to a group of college students?

Who would prefer to attend the rally, picnic, or barbecue type of event?

Who would lend most authority appearing with the candidate before the Chamber of Commerce, NAACP, or League of Women Voters?

Should a man, student, senior citizen or minority person accompany the candidate?

AIDE COMMITTEE CHAIR

The Aide Chair works closely at all times with the Scheduling Chair to help keep the candidate's busy 14-hour-a-day schedule working as smoothly as possible.

53

The duties of the Aide Committee Chair are to:

1. Recruit Aides from a variety of ages, interests and influence.

2. Plan and conduct training sessions which will include:

Information about the candidate's stand on issues and how she will manage them in question periods.

How to introduce the candidate to individuals, to groups.

How to make a fund-raising pitch.

How to make a speech soliciting workers, money, etc.

Methods for initiating and terminating discussion during appearances.

Methods for removing candidate graciously from "buttonholers."

Where and how to use campaign materials.

How to review with candidate weak and strong points of presentation.

3. In close cooperation with Scheduling Chair, plan all schedules for Aides. Calendar should be planned at least two weeks in advance.

4. Phone, a day or two before scheduled events, all contact persons to review times, places, addresses, numbers and types of people attending events and other pertinent data. (Scheduling Chair will make initial contacts and plans, but Aides Chair should follow up immediately prior to the event).

5. Prepare backup Aides list for cancellations. Find substitute Aide (or serve in that capacity) for such cancellations.

6. Prepare contents of Aide's packet of information. (See Packet section.)

7. Select and assign Aides for each day. See that the Aide is briefed about any special problems anticipated.

8. After assignment, collect packet from Aide, see that all lists, cards and monies are delivered to Headquarters Manager. Check for follow-up suggestions, recommendations, etc., and arrange to implement such suggestions.

9. Plan and schedule periodic Aide Committee meetings for technique refinement, form alterations, etc.

It is most efficient to arrange Aide assignment on a full day schedule whenever possible. One person who has the day's activities well in control, smoothly facilitates the busy candidate's movements from one event to another.

THE AIDE PACKET

The importance of the office preparation for the candidate's schedule of daily events cannot be sufficiently emphasized. The Aide's work in the field is backed by the office staff which has prepared the following packet of materials:

Typed schedule: Includes times, places, contact persons, local flavor data, telephone numbers, press contacts, etc.

55

Map and accurate directions to all destinations: Make sure in scheduling that adequate time is given for travel to and from events.

Clipboard sign-up sheets for those attending events; cards or check lists for volunteer workers; sign-ups for endorsements; lists of names, addresses and amounts from contributors.

Literature (brochures, flyers, issues sheets), bumper stickers, pins, balloons or other handouts. Make sure that there is adequate material for the numbers anticipated. Consider the kind of event and determine what type of materials will be best for that group. For example: where is the best place to hand out balloons; what literature is most appropriate for the Kiwanis luncheon; where is the best place to sell (or give) bumper stickers or pins?

Aides daily report form, which should include space for a list of persons who should receive a thank-you letter. It is important to make certain that all persons who have contributed time, money, talent or services be thanked for such efforts. Keeping up with the list of thank-yous on a day-to-day basis will facilitate the process. People are always pleased to receive recognition, and recognition within a reasonable amount of time is even more appreciated.

56 AUTHORIZATION FOR USE OF NAMES IN ADVERTISING

It is wise to begin gathering names for public endorsements very early in the campaign and to keep them on file for use in newspaper and other advertising endorsements closer to election day.

The advertising may be a general list of supporters, or a list such as "Doctors for Mary Doe for Assembly" or "Riverside Residents for Mary Doe."

Newspapers will insist that you have those signatures on file and will request to see them when you place advertising orders. This is to avoid legal complications if a name is used in the advertising and that person claims he/she has not endorsed the candidate. The signed card is there to prove the fact.

Getting Her Elected

You need the endorsers' signatures. Also ask that they print their names. People become

---

MARY DOE FOR ASSEMBLY

Name _____ Phone _____
(Print)
Address _____ City _____ Zip _____

Here is my contribution $ _____ Pledge $_____

I will work in the campaign:
(check area of interest and ability)

Advertising ____	Headqtr. Staff __	Transportation _____
Aide _____	Hostess: coffee __	Luncheon: fund-raiser _____
Clerical _____	Mailing _____	Registrar _____
Fund-Raising __	Precinct Work __	Research _____
Graphics _____	Telephone _____	Other _____

I authorize the use of my name for advertising purposes:

Print Name _____

Signature _____ Date

Sample Authorization Form

AIDE DAILY REPORT

Aide Name _____ Telephone _____

Comment _____

Date _____

Thank you list:

Name	Name
Address	Address
City, Zip	City, Zip
Date of event	Date of event
Service rendered	Service rendered
Thank you sent	Thank you sent

Sample Aide Report Form

angry when their names are misspelled but frequently their signatures are illegible. Ask for their address and city so you can be sure they reside in the district. A standard sheet of paper on a clipboard is one way to collect signatures at large gatherings. In addition, whenever possible, have people fill out a 3x5 card, so that it can be filed. Those cards may then be checked more easily for duplications, or verification of signatures.

The form should include this statement: "I authorize the use of my name for advertising purposes in support of Mary Doe, Assembly Candidate."

COFFEE HOST

58

Coffees are a good way to get a candidate around early in the campaign. They are usually neighborhood affairs, a circle of the host's friends, or a local organization. Morning and evening are preferred times for coffees, although the evening is best because then working men and women can attend.

Coffees are valuable in building a volunteer staff early and in getting recognition and support. Coffees have a good snowballing effect when a staff member is there to solicit and tie down offers of help. As the campaign continues, coffees are not as important as they are early in the campaign, unless large numbers of people (more than 50) will attend.

The Coffee Host should select a committee to assist with:

1. Telephoning invitations. As coffees are usually planned within a short time span, and mailed invitations cost money better put in the campaign kitty, a phone call from a friend is the best way to get a group together. The host should figure that one in three persons notified will attend. If the host wants twenty-five in attendance, then it is necessary to phone at least 75 persons. Remember that the call itself is publicity because the candidate's name is mentioned, and her appearance in the community is noted.

2. Preparing, serving refreshments.

3. Introducing the candidate when she arrives to other guests. The host, or someone in the group, should make the formal introduction to the candidate's speech. The host, or someone in the group, should make the fund-raising pitch also, as people are more willing to give money when a peer asks for it than when a stranger does.

59

If no one is willing to make a fund-raising pitch the group should not be made to feel uncomfortable about refusing. The Aide should be prepared to take over that function. The host should be informed that the candidate will appear about fifteen minutes after the announced beginning of the event, and that her presentation will last 15 or 20 minutes, followed by a question period of 15 minutes. The candidate should leave shortly after her presentation is terminated. The fund-raising pitch, request for workers, future hosts, endorsements, etc. should be made immediately after the candidate's presentation, before the interest and excitement of the group flags. Timing is important.

TELEPHONE COMMITTEE

The telephone is one of the major tools in a political campaign. If used effectively, the telephone campaign can be a great asset as it reflects the character of a candidate's organization and influences its reputation.

The telephone may be used to:

1. Conduct poll or survey.
2. Ask for money.
3. Canvass.
4. Invite potential supporters to a party or rally.
5. Identify potential supporters who need to register to vote.
6. Recruit workers.
7. Get-out-the-vote.

60

Telephoning may be done by volunteers at home or at the headquarters where a number of phones are installed and used many hours a day. A telephoner working seven hours a day on a 15-second call (reminding those on a well-prepared list of names and numbers to vote) can reach 200 people a day. Each call in a phone survey will take about a minute to complete.

A pleasant-sounding voice, projecting enthusiasm and knowledge, is an essential. Courtesy, a straightforward approach and a good listening ability are all important to an effective telephone campaign.

Training sessions should be planned in advance, and all committee members should have an opportunity to perfect their telephone techniques.

TELEPHONE TECHNIQUE

It is essential to determine the needs of the person being called. The time of day to call must be considered, and the prospect should be asked if it is convenient to talk.

The reason for the call should be clearly stated. The caller must understand the reason, put it into simple language, and transmit this to the person called.

The specific steps in a telephone call are: **61**

1. Introduce yourself.

2. Give the reason for the call.

3. Mention the advantage of the call to the person being called. (Brief, remember-to-vote type of call will terminate here with thank-you and good-bye.)

4. Find out if it is convenient to talk at this time. (If inconvenient, pin down a convenient time and terminate.)

5. Ask questions that will encourage interest. (Exchange ideas, discuss needs, discover local interests.)

6. If objections are raised, listen to them and be understanding. However . . . restate your reason and need for calling.

7. Restate all arrangements, agreements for clarification.

8. Thank person for time taken.

9. Say good-bye.

10. Allow other party to hang up first.

The three main parts of the telephone presentation are:

1. Explain what is to be suggested.

Example: Vote for Candidate/Solicit money/Have a Coffee.

2. Explain why suggestion is being made.

Example: Help get party slate elected/Bring candidate in contact with a new group of voters.

3. Ask for action (unless a survey).

Example: If suggestion is to vote for candidate, give choice of action. "Do you have transportation to the polls, or can we provide it?" Or, "You have agreed to support with money. Can we pick up your check or will you mail it?"

The three main objections you may encounter are:

1. I have no time.
2. I have no interest.
3. I'm not sure right now.

Listen to the objection; recognize it by agreeing with it, for example, "Yes, I understand how busy working mothers are, however . . ." Then restate the purpose in another manner. Ask for action on a more minor level. For example, "If you cannot hold a coffee at this time, will you contact a friend who will hold a coffee?"

TELEPHONE COMMITTEE CHAIR

The responsibilities of the Telephone Chairperson (in cooperation with Personnel Coordinator and/or Headquarters Manager) are to:

1. Recruit Telephone Committee workers.

2. Develop telephone campaign plans.

3. Work out pitch, names and numbers to be called.

4. Conduct training sessions for committee members.

5. Set up time schedules for task completion.

6. Distribute work to committee members and follow up to see if task is completed in allotted time.

7. Collect and organize all information derived from telephone campaign.

63

TRANSPORTATION COMMITTEE

The main task of the Transportation Committee will be on primary and general election days when voters need to be driven to and from polls. At other times, transportation needs may include driving people to and from picnics, rallies and other places where they will meet the candidate. Or the Transportation Committee may be called upon to distribute posters and literature. But the main work is on election day.

TRANSPORTATION CHAIR

The Transportation Chairperson works directly under the Precinct Chair and in close cooperation with the Headquarters Manager.

The duties of the Transportation Chair are to:

1. Determine the transportation needs during the campaign, in cooperation with the Precinct Chair and Get-Out-The-Vote Chair.

2. Select a house in every precinct, with a phone number that can be advertised, where people needing transportation may call. Drivers will get their assignments from this house, and contact with main headquarters will be maintained.

3. Recruit a minimum of one driver per precinct. You can determine whether additional drivers are needed if the area houses more senior citizens, people at the poverty level, or has great distance to polling place.

4. Work with Telephone Chair to conduct a telephone canvass of transportation needs. Unless the telephone numbers for transportation are known to the voter, it will do little good to have a system set up. A list of numbers to call in each precinct should be included in a newspaper ad a day or two before election. Literature which is distributed the week before election should have those numbers prominently displayed. Also telephone canvassers should give out the number when they do their canvassing.

5. Coordinate with other candidates and party headquarters. Efforts should be combined to avoid duplication, to enlist greater numbers of workers for party support and to encourage good will at times when emotions run high.

6. Maintain lists of drivers, precinct house headquarters, and telephone canvassers.

Research

There is nothing more shattering to a candidate, or to the campaign, than to find she is ignorant of an issue important to the people she is addressing, or that she is oblivious to local problems which require a particular perspective. The candidate who takes a stand and backs it up with facts and figures is going to have a better chance of being taken seriously than the candidate who does not do her homework.

It is frequently assumed by the public that a man knows what he is talking about because he has had business or professional experience that gives him prior knowledge about how it all works. The same attitude does not go for a woman. Therefore, she must be prepared to prove herself to the constituency. The knowledge she demonstrates, the ease and fluency with which she fields questions, the content and quality of her speeches are going to make a difference in her being accepted as a serious office seeker — as a leader.

Naturally, the candidate will develop a style of presentation which best suits her. Personality and charisma will be great assets, but without hard information and facts, which are the foundation of any campaign, those assets alone will not suffice.

The candidate will not have time or energy to accumulate and digest all the information necessary for the campaign. For this reason, the kind of research attempted and its utilization in the campaign will be important. Major decisions on issues or strategy may be critically influenced by the presence or absence of pertinent, reliable information.

The range of campaign research may include:

Issues

The two or three major issues of the campaign must be determined and researched in depth. A preliminary *issues survey* may be valuable in determining what those major topics will be and how they will be developed. There also will be a number of lesser issues which will be of concern to certain groups of voters. Position papers may be prepared for distribution to interested voters and to the media. They must be prepared with the candidate's participation and full understanding and they should be reviewed frequently.

Local Concerns

How identifiable groups view the controversial issues; what ramifications state or national events have at the local level; and how groups; change their attitudes and opinions as the campaign develops, are areas that should be covered by the research.

Legislation

Past, present and pending legislation which affects local voters, as well as party platform stands, must be known to the candidate.

69

Opponent's Record

The personal and voting history of the opponent, his/her financial backers, and recent community activities must be at the fingertips.

Precinct Research

Census data, previous election returns, precinct targeting and canvassing assessments and voter registration lists must all be analyzed. (See chapter on Precinct Organization).

Political Poll (Survey)

Surveys can and should do more than tell which candidate is ahead at what stage of the campaign. A well-designed, well-conducted *voter preference poll* (probability sample survey) can reveal:

1. The issues concerning groups identified by age, education and income levels, ethnic origin, sex, marital status and geographic location.

2. The willingness of these groups to vote for women candidates.

' 3. How voters perceive the candidate's stand on issues and the candidate's general image.

4. The degree of satisfaction with the incumbent or the political party in power.

5. How identifiable groups respond to current controversial issues.

6. When, where and to whom political literature should be sent.

7. Who the undecided voters are and what they see as issues.

If your campaign can afford to hire a professional survey firm, that is the best way to go. Ten to fifteen percent of the budget might be expended on research. The next best thing to hiring a good firm is to hire a professional consultant to assist at the planning and computer stages. If you are unable to afford even that kind of professional help, make sure your poll meets professional standards as closely as possible.

There are several kinds of surveys which you may conduct:

Household interviews of respondents in their own homes.

Telephone surveys using the same selection techniques as utilized in household interviews, but more efficient in terms of time and money.

Mail surveys (return postcard) which is the least efficient in terms of time, money and percentage of response.

Informal surveys conducted at shopping centers or high pedestrian-traffic areas. This is probably the easiest to conduct, but the least reliable.

Once you have decided what you want to find out, and who you want to find out from, a sample design must be set up. The size of the sample is, of course, determined by the size of the electorate. A district with under 10,000 voters may require a sample of 150, while one with over 100,000 voters may require a sample of 800.

71

The questionnaire you prepare must have precise language and proper sequencing so that the respondent clearly understands what is being asked. If you must rely on volunteers to interview the sample, make sure they have solid training sessions before they interview. If you cannot conduct a survey in a professional manner, you are better off to forget it. The data you get with inadequate selection techniques and a poor questionnaire may hurt your campaign rather than help it.

The techniques of surveying, interviewing and statistical and analysis are too complicated for inclusion here. There are very good books on the subject. You may also obtain information about this research area by writing to the U.S. Government Printing Office, Washington, D.C., and to the U.S. Executive Office of the President, Bureau of the Budget, as well as the regional offices of the U.S. Bureau of Labor Statistics. A university in your area also may be a source of professional expertise.

72

VOTER PREFERENCE POLL

Goal: To assess _____(candidate's) chances of being elected to (Senate / Assembly / Congress / Governor).
Voting information will be categorized according to:

Males
Females
Age Groups
Income Groups
Education Level Groups
Marital Status
Party Affiliation
Geographic Location

73

Information gathered will indicate:

Whether a woman can be elected to this office.

Which of the potential candidates has the greatest name identification among the listed groups.

The degree to which candidates are known or unknown in different communities.

What the important issues are to each of the different groups, listed above.

Sample Voter Preference Poll

I.   "Pardon me. Are you a registered voter in _____County?"
(If "no," find another subject to interview.)
(If "yes," check: _____male _____female.)

"We are conducting a political poll in the _____
Congressional/Senatorial/Assembly District.

I'd like to ask you some questions which will only take a few
minutes of your time."

II.   "We are interested in knowing what you think are the most
important issues in your community."   (Show list.)

"What do you think are the two most important issues?"

1._____ 2._____

III. "I'm going to read you the names of people who are in politics.

Do you recognize any of these names? Who?"_____

_____

_____

"What does he/she do?" _____

IV. "Do you think a Chicano candidate has a chance of being elected?"
Yes_____ No_____

"Do you think a black candidate has a chance of being elected?"
Yes _____ No_____

"Do you think a woman candidate has a chance of being elected?"
Yes _____ No_____

"Would you personally feel comfortable voting for a woman for
the state Legislature/U.S. Congress/the Senate?

"Is there some woman you would vote for?"   Yes____ No_____

"What is her name?" _____

DATE_____LOCATION_____INTERVIEWER_____

(Turn paper over and hand it to interviewee.)

V.   "Will you please fill out the confidential information
      on this side?"

      "After you have checked the appropriate age, income, marital
      status, education, and party affiliation, please fold your
      paper and put it in this folder (or sealed box)."

      "Thank you very much for participating in this voter
      preference poll."

VOTER PREFERENCE POLL

CONFIDENTIAL

AGE: ____18 - 25   ____26 - 35   ____36 - 45   ____46 & over

MARITAL STATUS:
        ____Married   ____Single   ____Widowed   ____Divorced

INCOME:
        ____Under $5,000   ____$5,000 - 10,000   ____21,000 - 40,000

        ____Student   ____11,000 - 20,000   ____Over 40,000

EDUCATION:
        ____Less than high school   ____Some college

        ____Some high school   ____College degree

        ____High school graduate

POLITICAL PARTY AFFILIATION:

        ____Democrat   ____American Independent party

        ____Republican   ____Vote independently

        ____Peace & Freedom   ____Decline to state

INSTRUCTIONS FOR VOTER
PREFERENCE SURVEY

Each interviewer will complete 30 *Voter Preference Poll Surveys,* using the preceding form or a similar one your staff develops.

Before each interview, make sure the interviewer fills in the date of the interview, location, and his/her initials on the form.

Interview only registered voters.

Prior to the interviewing, your staff will determine ten issues which are current concerns of the electorate. These ten issues will be typed clearly in a list to be used in the interviews.

The staff will also type a list of persons known in political circles. The list should include the name of your candidate and her opponents, in both the primary and general elections.

During the survey, the interviewee will supply his/her own answers to Sections I, IV, and V.

For Section II, the interviewer will hand the list of ten issues to the interviewee. If the interviewee wishes to name an issue not on the list, write that issue in the space allocated.

In Section III, the interviewer will *read* the list of names to the interviewee.

The interviewee will then complete the confidential information on the reverse side, fold the survey, and place it in the folder or sealed box. (The interviewer should not fold or deposit the surveys, in order to assure the person being interviewed of confidentiality.)

Always thank participants for their cooperation.

RESEARCH COORDINATOR

The duties of the Research Coordinator are to:

1. Serve as a member of the Executive Staff, working under the direction of the Campaign Manager.

2. Determine the master plan for research activities, the initial kinds of research projects and surveys, and the general time line for completion.

3. Assist in the selection of the survey firm or consultant.

77

4. Work closely with Advisory Committee early in campaign.

5. Recruit research teams. Delegate tasks, time limits, and supervise completion of the tasks.

6. Set up a filing and distribution system regarding materials for staff members, with a continual updating process for media and other staff needs. *(Research which remains in the file has no value.)*

7. Serve as liaison with Congressional offices, state party headquarters, and Senate/Assembly Caucus for materials and information.

8. Assist the Precinct Coordinator in the de-

sign, assignment and completion of all precinct research needs.

9. Recruit an Historian and delegate all clippings and scrapbook activities to that person.

ADVISORY COMMITTEE

An Advisory Commitee should be selected well in advance of the campaign. The committee should not number more than four persons. They will be selected because they are persons with a good knowledge of the district from a practical and political standpoint.

Their role is to identify the concerns of special interest groups and to serve as a sounding board for early campaign strategies. They will not be decision-makers or even be part of the decision-making process. Instead, they will supply a broad range of attitudes and points of view which are found throughout the community. They will help clarify issues and will focus on ideas for treating special problems which come up.

The Advisory Committee also can be very helpful by making suggestions for recruiting key workers, fund-raisers, and contributors. They can give valuable insight or assistance in getting support and endorsements from business, labor and professional organizations. In preference to a regular schedule, they should be called together when needed, or on an individual basis. The Committee will be utilized more often in the early part of the campaign, but less frequently as things progress. The Legal Advisor may also be a member of this group.

The Campaign Manager will work closely with the Advisory Committee. The Research Coordinator may get basic research ideas for surveys and polls from Advisory Committee members.

For other information gathering purposes, the Research Coordinator should find individuals in the community who can give valuable information from their particular professional or interest fields. Research Committee members will then interview these individuals and make notes on their comments. If some of the individuals have a great deal of expertise on a particular subject, a briefing session should be set up with them and the candidate. Sometimes people who are asked to give information will also give advice on how to run the campaign. If possible, the candidate should be spared from this kind of a session.

79

Good advisors, researchers and consultants can be:

1. College and university students who are accustomed to researching in depth, giving attention to detail.

2. High school, college and university instructors and professors.

3. Elected public officials, past or present.

4. Minority group leaders.

5. Labor union leaders.

6. Members or leaders of community organizations (citizen action, environment, school bond, tax initiative, etc.).

LEGAL ADVISOR

The responsibilities of the Legal Advisor are:

1. See that all papers are properly filed and that all legal requirements are met.

2. Review all campaign literature for libelous statements.

3. Review all opponent's literature for libelous statements.

4. Work with Finance Coordinator and Treasurer to see that all contributions reports meet legal requirements.

80

5. Serve as an advisor when legal questions, such as contracts for services, come before the staff.

Political Party Structure and Coordination

At the top of the political party structure is the national party committee, which conducts the national convention where party presidential and vice presidential candidates are selected.

81

Both the Democratic and Republican parties have a central committee in each state. The chair of the state central committee is empowered to direct party activities and to be a unifying and coordinating force for all the organizations working for the party. The state committee's activities may include:

Precinct organization.
Candidate search and support.
State convention organization.
Money-raising to finance party activities.
State party platform determination.

In most counties of the country each political party has a county central committee as part of the state party structure. It performs the same functions at the local level as state central committees do at the state level.

Unless the candidate has been active in party politics at the state or local level (and it is helpful to have been), one of the first things she must do is attend her party's county central committee meetings. It is very important to know how the committee operates, and to know the central committee members. Initiative such as this on her part is necessary, as party organizations do not usually seek out and encourage women to run for office. Cooperation of the local party organization is important not only in what it may be able to do for her campaign, but also in what it can't (or won't) do for her campaign.

The party committees are not supposed to endorse candidates in the primary because the whole purpose of a primary election is to allow the voters to select the party's nominee. Of course, the individual central committee members will be biased in favor of a personal choice for nominee and often individually endorse that choice.

Staff members also should establish a good relationship with the county committee early. A list of committee members and the time and place of meetings should be available from the County Board of Elections. If you campaign in more than one county, you will need to establish communications with the central committees in all counties.

The local and state party chairpersons will have information about state and national party officials who will be visiting your area and organizing events around their visits. Your candidate should attend these functions whenever possible.

Coordination and cooperation between same-party candidates is very important in precinct work as well. As soon as the primary is over, you must decide how, when and where you want to be part of the party slate. Communications with other candidates and their staffs should be open.

One of the most important functions of the central committee is party precinct organization. They will be organizing and coordinating voter registration, canvassing, telephoning, leafleting and precinct walking. It will be necessary for you to determine how your campaign workers will cooperate in those activities.

83

Ways the central committees may assist in your campaign:

1. Keep your staff advised of party calendar for your candidate's inclusion in all events.

2. See that your materials are displayed and distributed at headquarters and party functions.

3. Contribute money to your campaign after the primary.

4. Include you in slate mailers and other slate materials.

5. Include your materials and workers in all precincting plans.

Once your candidate is the nominee, the central committee, by law, may not publicly support the candidate from the opposing party. However, you should not expect positive support to just happen.

You will have to convince the party members of your candidate's qualifications. Because most people who work at local party levels are accustomed to seeing women in the lesser roles within the political structure, they may resent and consider your candidate presumptuous. Male candidates appearing on the ticket may feel embarrassment unless they are convinced that your candidate is qualified. The party may have some reservations about giving a woman candidate the same amount of money they normally give to male candidates. They will more than likely have assessed your candidate's chances of winning as less than the male candidate's.

There are other state and local party clubs and organizations which are often active in support of candidates. Your county central committee will have a list of the party-affiliated organizations in your area.

84

Media

More and more elections are being won or lost through the use of the media: newspaper, radio and television promotion. It is not unusual for an advertising firm to be hired to "package" the candidate for sale in much the same manner that soap is packaged and sold. Because effective use of the media is an integral and costly part of the campaign, whenever possible, professional people should be hired in preference to amateur volunteers.

Studies repeatedly show that it is the *image* which inspires the voter sufficiently to cast a ballot for the candidate. That image often exists in spite of the candidate's stand on issues, qualifications, merit, ability or intelligence. In that a candidate is not able to meet personally with even a third of the voters, she must rely on media to do the job for her. The goal is to get the candidate known by as many people as possible and to inspire the confidence necessary for the vote.

What the image is and how it is projected will be important from the very start. You must try to achieve a strong balance in the character qualities you want to project. A woman candidate must be shown as assertive rather than aggressive, attractive without being a sexpot, self-confident but not domineering. She must neither be too pushy nor show reticence. The human qualities of compassion and sympathy must not resemble emotionality. Because society tends to label active women as pushy, aggressive, domineering or masculine, voters may be more ready to see negative traits in a woman candidate than they will in a man candidate. They may perceive determined women as shrill, strident or emotional. A woman is easily discounted by being labeled "just one of those women's libbers."

A good media campaign can help a woman candidate project the necessary image. It will also help establish the name identification and recognition that are crucial on election day.

Most voters, when asked, will have only a vague idea of who their congressman or senator is, what he does, or how well he is doing it. They will tend to vote for the incumbent, partly because they recognize his name when they see it.

Another factor which favors incumbency is that the incumbent candidate has the distinction of being *the* congressman, *the* senator or *the* assemblyman. He is able to speak from this vantage point and have entree to the media and to many events which are closed to the challenger. A good media campaign will help neutralize that advantage.

MEDIA SURVEY

You must learn early and well how to use the media to communicate with people in the district. The *first step* is to conduct a media survey:

Determine the dominant media vehicle in the district. Do voters use radio, television or newspapers most often? Which stations and what papers?

87

What part of the electorate does each medium reach? The stations and newspapers themselves can give you a profile of their patrons.

The *second step* is to list all the radio and TV stations (network, independent and cable), and all the daily, weekly, college and giveaway newspapers. Determine the names, addresses and phone numbers of all the key news contact persons, the daily and/or weekly deadlines for submitting material, the bias of the station or paper, and how they like the material prepared. Advertising rates and contact persons should be collected at the same time and listed separately.

Once you have finished this research you should be able to determine what media, or combination, will be most useful in the campaign. If your survey demonstrates that radio reaches more people than newspapers, you will emphasize radio more. However, if you find that a particular newspaper reaches a segment of the voting population you need to influence (i.e., senior citizens, homeowners, working-class people, etc.) then your media strategy will include that newspaper when and where it will be most effective.

THE FREE MEDIA CAMPAIGN

The survey should also give the key to using free media. That usage in combination with the paid media campaign should be designed for the maximum candidate exposure.

Remember that all the news media will be interested in your campaign activities: the issues which your candidate discusses, where she will be appearing, comments about her opponent's record and her ideas for positive programs. She is news merely by being a candidate.

Make the best of media interest by offering newsworthy items. When you call a press conference make sure your candidate has something important to say. Do not repeat news items that already passed across news desks that morning.

If you phone the local radio station offering a short comment, prepare an item of interest to that radio audience. If you seek a TV interview

88

for the evening news presentation, prepare an observation that is timely and presents a different point of view. Most of the personnel in the media will give you as much free time as they can if your presentation is dynamic and your material has specific news merit.

The first contact with media people will be vital to the campaign. Very early the candidate should make appointments with all of the key people on the media survey list. If a Press Secretary has been selected he/she should accompany the candidate on the first visit. Take this opportunity to present the candidate, her staff members and the campaign. Also use the opportunity to get to know the reporters, editors and broadcasters. These are the professional people who are the base of the communications system. They know the community and the issues; they can help make or break a candidate. If your opponent is a more established, well-known person it may be impossible to convince the media to support your candidate. However, with a professional media campaign, you can at least see that your candidate is taken seriously.

89

Realize that media people can be open and interested or they can be racist, sexist and bigoted just like the rest of the population. They can give your candidate fair treatment or ignore her or present her in a devastating way. They can print flattering or unflattering pictures.

For example, two instructors from the same college, a man and a woman, campaigned for the same office in a primary. Articles about their

debates and opposing campaigns were head-
lined:

"WOMEN'S LIBBER
TAKES ON PROFESSOR" and
"COLLEGE INSTRUCTOR
ATTACKED BY FEMINIST."

She was always characterized as a feminist
radical, and few people realized from the news
coverage that both candidates were at the same
professional level at the same educational institu-
tion.

On the other hand, media people can respect your candidate as qualified and competent
with a professional staff and organization. They
will if they find your candidate and your material
knowledgeable and newsworthy. A good first
impression and continuing communication with
media people is essential.

Subscribe to all of the newspapers in the
district. The Press Secretary or a member of the
media team should read all of them and mark
items of particular interest to the candidate. Daily, the candidate must at least glance through
these items.

Members of the media team should also
monitor local radio and television programs. It is
essential that you know what is reported and
how. It is also important to know how much and
what kind of free publicity your opponent is
getting. If it is more than you are getting, you
may need to review your strategy and your rela-

tionship with media people. You may have to demand equal treatment.

The media survey has provided the basis for obtaining free publicity through news releases, press conferences, radio spots, television news and issues programs. You should deliver a biography (resume) and an 8 x 10 glossy picture of the candidate as early in the campaign as possible to all contacts. Include brochures and handouts. The Press Secretary then should maintain regular contact with key media persons.

News Releases

Hand deliver *news releases* on local issues or major campaign positions as often as you have something new and worthwhile to say. Minimize routine items. Observe deadlines.

91

Since editors and reporters must read a great amount of material daily, the first lines of the news release should include *who, what, why, where, when* and *how*. Make sure it is timely and hard news.

The release should be typed, double spaced, on only one side of the paper. Send copies, not carbon, to everyone on the list.

Never play favorites. See that everyone has equal access to the candidate and the material.

The news release should look like this:

BETTY JOANS FOR STATE SENATE
2222 MAIN STREET
MIDTOWN, CALIFORNIA   97942
Contact: MARY SMITH, Press Secretary
466-1122 or 466-2244
Date: June 1, 19--
FOR IMMEDIATE RELEASE:

Betty Joans, State Senate candidate,

announced today that she would per-

sonally visit the women's jail facili-

ties to observe the conditions . . .

92

-- more --

JOANS FOR SENATE   PAGE 2

Joans has received numerous complaints

from inmates about the deplorable . . .

END

Press Conference

The *press conference* is an excellent way to get coverage from the maximum number of media representatives. Press conferences are called for the following reasons:

1. The candidate will announce a major decision, program, or position that can be explored by questions from the press.

2. An issue will be discussed which has been requested by a number of newspeople, or is an obvious issue of the day and the candidate's point view will be newsworthy.

Notify *all* media about the press conference as soon as your plans are completed. The best time is between 8:30 and 10 a.m. for afternoon papers and evening newscasters. But play fair with the morning papers and broadcasters by scheduling some p.m. press conferences. Conferences are often held near or in government centers. They also may be held in a hotel conference room. If the candidate is going to speak about a jail or a childcare facility, you may want to hold the conference at the site.

93

A news release containing all of the material the candidate will discuss should be prepared in advance and handed out to those attending the press conference. The Press Secretary (or a well-known supporter) should introduce the candidate, and be available to handle other details. Coffee may be served if convenient and customary in the area.

Radio

Radio is an often overlooked but important way to reach people who are otherwise unreachable. Statistics show that many people never see a daily newspaper, nor do they watch television, but they do listen to the radio. People who remain at home or work at routine jobs often listen to the radio for long hours. A prime radio time is during the morning and evening commute when large numbers of people are trapped in their cars with the radio on.

Radio consistently beats newspapers and television to the day's news items through the early morning newscast. Frequently a short spot on the early morning radio news will become a feature on the evening television program.

94

There are two ways to get your material to the radio newscaster:

1. The Press Secretary can call the station around 7 a.m. and ask if they would like a statement from the candidate on some issue currently in the news. If accepted, the candidate comes on the phone and makes a 30- to 45-second, clear, concise statement which is recorded right then over the phone.

2. The candidate can tape the statement, either late the previous night or very early in the morning, and have the tape delivered to the radio station before the morning newscast.

Another means of good radio exposure is a "talk" or "call-in" radio show. Not only does this afford wide coverage, but a call-in show gives the radio audience an opportunity to question the candidate, and to hear the candidate deal with issues in a conversational manner. Prior to scheduling the candidate on one of these programs, staff persons should monitor the program to determine how the program host deals with guests, how questions are asked, what some of the biases of the host are, and what the interests of the radio audience are.

Television

Reaching the *television* newscaster is similar to reaching the radio newsperson. Both need to be contacted early in the morning and asked if they are interested in the candidate's comment. Television is different in that the candidate must be where the TV camera is, and the candidate must look as good as possible. Candidate comments on an issue should be less than 60 seconds, and the background should be as interesting as possible. Frequently, TV shots are done out-of-doors in natural light. Television news programs usually are shown from 4:30 to 7 p.m., but the TV tapes must be made before early afternoon to allow time for editing.

95

Most local TV stations have local issues programs of a half-hour duration. They are most often shown on the weekend at something less than prime time. The candidate should be scheduled on those programs whenever possible to speak on issues of the campaign, as well as on issues in her area of expertise or professional background.

THE PAID MEDIA CAMPAIGN

If the campaign has enough money, a professional advertising agency should be hired. The "Standard Directory of Advertising Agencies" contains listings of agencies in every state. Shop around to get comparative rates for the services provided and the quality of work. Talk to people who have used the agencies in the past, especially for political campaigns.

Some of the questions you will want to ask a professional agency are:

1. Does the media the campaign will be dealing with really reach the audience we want to reach?

2. What will be the cost of advertising per person or per thousand persons reached?

3. What is the best kind of time and space for us to buy, based on the above research?

4. When should we advertise? What is the best saturation timing for the campaign?

These same questions will apply whether or not you can afford a professional agency. If your media budget is limited, try to buy professional services (or find volunteers) for some of these important specifics:

1. Advertising research and survey to answer the above questions.

2. Developing the major issues and theme of the campaign.

3. Layout and design of campaign materials and newspaper ads.

4. Preparing paid TV and radio spots.

Some of the advantages and disadvantages of the various media are:

Television

Very expensive, especially in prime time. Make sure that the viewing audience is composed of people who live in your district and can vote for your candidate. If you decide to use television, start collecting good action films and still shots of your candidate and campaign activities early. Most television advertising is purchased well in advance, and the saturation time is just prior to election.

Radio Advertising

A less expensive way to go, and often reaches your constituency with greater accuracy. That makes it practical for a low-budget campaign. Short 30-second to one minute spots can be used and should be purchased early for the best time slots. The candidate's name should be mentioned at least three times in every spot.

Newspaper Advertising

Newspapers charge more for political advertising than they do for regular advertising. Be sure to research the circulation . . . it may be larger than you want and you will be paying to reach people outside of your district. You can buy newspaper ads on shorter notice than either TV or radio time, but it is best not to wait too long. Competition from all candidates is very heavy the week prior to the election.

Other Campaign Literature

This is part of the paid media campaign and includes brochures, flyers, leaflets, bumper stickers, posters, placards, banners, balloons, hats and on down the list of campaign gimmicks.

The following is a list of tasks for materials preparation:

1. Select a photographer. You will need both a formal studio portrait as well as action shots. (See Photographer section.)

2. Choose the one picture which will be *the* campaign photo. Print at least two dozen 4 x 6 glossies. Enlarge (18 x 24) another dozen.

3. Select the colors, type of print, paper quality and design for all campaign materials. The same colors, etc., should be duplicated on all of the campaign materials so that there is an association with the candidate through coordinated materials.

4. Select key issues and phrases you will use on all the literature.

5. Determine the priority list of materials, the time each will be used in the campaign and the amounts of each that will be needed. It is very disheartening to attend a September picnic with many people who are turned on to your campaign and asking for bumper stickers or posters and to have to confess you are out of them. They are disappointed and you appear unprepared. It

98

is equally disappointing to have boxes of beautiful materials left in your garage in November. Establish early your need and priorities for the following:

A good brochure which contains the picture of the candidate, action shots, key issues, platform statements and all headquarters addresses and phone numbers. It should be attractive, informative and ready to be mailed or hand distributed.

Bumper stickers.

Small flyer cards with picture and compact information.

Buttons (pins) with a catchy phrase and candidate's name.

99

Balloons, with candidate's name and the office for which she is campaigning. These are great for picnics, barbecues, parades, rallies. You will also need a helium tank, string, scissors and people to fill and tie the balloons.

Posters.

Placards. They are often similar to posters, but are made of plastic or metal so they can withstand being out of doors for a long period of time.

Other materials as money and taste allow.

It cannot be overstated that *time* is absolutely essential in a good materials campaign. Design, artwork, photography, and layout production take talent, time and coordination. Printers' schedules must also be coordinated in the process. Since it is the campaign image which will be projected through the materials, it is better to have no materials than poor materials. What the literature looks like and how effectively it gets to the voter will be a measure of the candidate's ability to do a job well.

Distribution is another equally important factor which needs planning and coordination. How material is distributed, its prominence, style and noticeability will impress people as to the organizational ability of the candidate. An entire neighborhood putting candidate placards on their front lawns on a designated date is very effective. Posters which suddenly appear everywhere bring the candidate's name and face to the voter's attention. A large event such as a rally where balloons, pins, posters and literature are evident everywhere, with pleasant people distributing them, will make a great impression. That kind of materials management and effect takes a great deal of timing and coordination.

100

Direct Mail

A final aspect of the paid media campaign is direct mail contact with voters. *Direct computerized mail* can be a very useful communication vehicle in elections where more than 50,000 votes are cast. In smaller campaigns the use of a computer letter that looks like a hand-typed letter, individually addressed, may be very effective.

There are companies that will sell you computer lists of household addresses of home own-ers registered to vote. Or lists can be prepared for various ethnic, religious, or income level people who voted in the previous election. It is thus possible to deliver a special letter or brochure with a message specifically aimed at that particu-lar group of voters.

As with any other service, the campaign should shop around for a reliable computer company, one that has had some experience with political campaigns.

MEDIA COORDINATOR

Paid media may well represent the largest item in the budget. The Media Coordinator should be an individual who has had experience in newspaper, radio or television work, as well as a knowledge of advertising and materials prep-aration. Previous political experience is a big advantage, too. The Media Coordinator should be a person who can help project the candidate's image, and do it through all of the media.

101

The duties of the Media Coordinator are to:

1. Serve as a member of the Executive Staff under the direction of the Campaign Manager.

2. Recruit the Campaign Materials Chair and Advertising Chair.

3. Assist in the hiring of the Press Secretary and the Photographer.

4. Plan, with the Campaign Manager, the details and budget of the paid media campaign

which will include newspaper, radio, TV advertising and materials.

5. Supervise all aspects of the media campaign.

PRESS SECRETARY

The person who handles the press for the campaign is one of the most important people on the staff, second only to the Campaign Manager. This should be considered a full-time, paid professional assignment.

The Press Secretary is the person who writes and releases all news items to the newspapers, radio and TV. This person should have access to all media personnel within the district and should know how their systems work and what the hierarchy is. Good press relations are important to insure a good amount of coverage, and also the content and quality of it.

Many women candidates get coverage that is not what it should be. Too often, they are relegated to the society page or are described in less than favorable terms. An example is "Candidate Mary Doe, wife and mother . . ." while you never hear "Candidate John Doe, husband and father . . ."! I was described as "the blue-eyed mother of three" when I spoke on a significant subject. I never saw any description of my opponent such as "the balding, childless senator." A good Press Secretary will have to work for fair and equal treatment.

Another problem which may arise is the one presented by so-called "women's issues." Reporters will frequently question only on the issue of women's lib, rather than on other issues which the candidate may raise. The candidate's stand on education finance is less interesting from a news point of view compared to her stand on free-love, abortion, or other more heady social issues. So, your candidate's campaign credibility will have to be earned in the women's issue arena. Whoever handles your press should be prepared to handle this problem if it arises.

During my campaign I had two professional male journalists work, at different times, as my Press Secretary. Each also had previous political experience working for male candidates. They were angered and frustrated because 80% of the press releases they put out, which they felt would have been printed in ordinary circumstances, were ignored. They both began to realize what sex discrimination was. They also noticed a lot of hostility and condescension toward the campaign on the part of male reporters and editors with whom they worked.

103

The duties of the Press Secretary are to:

1. Serve as a member of the Executive Staff.

2. Set up a press file including newspapers, radio and television stations, with names of contact editors, reporters, commentators, etc. Include addresses, phone numbers, pertinent data, deadlines, etc.

3. Personally meet with key contact persons in the media.

4. Make certain that every newspaper, radio

and television station in the district has the candidate's biography (resume) and at least one glossy photo of *the* campaign picture of the candidate. Material should include the name of the Press Secretary, headquarter's address and phone number.

5. Plan and carry out a free media strategy.

6. Write releases, see that appropriate photos, other data are included and mailed or delivered as needed.

7. Set up appointments for interviews, commentaries, visits to editors, TV and radio stations.

8. Call press conferences for important candidate announcements and statements.

104

9. Keep close track of what's happening in the district, with the opponent, and in the campaign.

ADVERTISING CHAIR

The Advertising Chair will plan and design (under the direction of the Media Coordinator) the content, type, quality and amount of all paid advertising in newspaper, radio and television. An individual who has some background in the advertising field as well as in radio, TV or newspaper work would be desirable.

The duties of the Advertising Chair are to:

1. Research the audience each newspaper, radio and television station will reach.

2. Research newspaper, television and

radio advertising costs and regulations.

3. Prepare the ad layouts for newspaper advertising.

4. Prepare the spot tapes for radio advertising.

5. Prepare the film, slide or poster spots for television advertising.

6. Purchase time as authorized by Campaign Manager.

7. See that advertising is completed as per contract with media.

CAMPAIGN MATERIALS CHAIR

The Campaign Materials Chair, working under the direction of the Media Coordinator, is the person who has responsibility for the overall design and layout of campaign materials. Campaign materials may include brochures, bumper stickers, buttons, balloons, posters, placards, etc.

105

Design, color, type of print, and other technical details are the Materials Chair's responsibility. Therefore, the job should be placed in the hands of someone who has had experience in the field of advertising design and layout. There are advertising firms in some communities which will handle all of this aspect of the campaign.

If the work is kept within the campaign structure, *the duties of the Materials Chair are to:*

1. Determine, with the Media Coordinator, kinds, style, colors, type and general content of campaign materials.

2. Make up layouts (with approval) for such materials.

3. Research cost of production and determine amounts needed and when needed.

4. Place orders, see thay are completed at agreed times and in agreed amounts.

PHOTOGRAPHER

There will be a need for a professional, studio portrait of the candidate. As there is a trend away from the posed photo to the less formal, action type of picture, have both kinds of photographic work done. Do it early so that you will have an opportunity to assess what type of picture best projects the candidate's image and so the candidate can become accustomed to being photographed.

One picture should be selected as *the* campaign photo. Unless the candidate's face is already well known to many voters in the district, one picture which is repeated on all material will give her a stronger identity. Various shots of the candidate doing different kinds of things are colorful and add interest to campaign material, but the repetition of the one photograph will gain more voter recognition over a period of months.

Voters are also interested in the candidate's family, and, if the candidate is female, they will be especially interested. If your candidate has a family, give deep thought about how she will be pictured with them. One young woman discovered that there was great concern among voters about who would care for her pre-school-age children if she were elected. Because she came across as the mother of small children rather than as a capable and able woman, she found it best to discontinue showing pictures of herself with little ones.

A campaign photographer is also needed when the candidate is meeting with other impor-tant personages or attending a local function. You cannot depend on the local news photo-grapher to picture your candidate in the most flattering manner, or even to include her in the shot with the visiting dignitary. One unique prob-lem a woman may have is height. When I was told to stand close while talking to a visiting 6'2'' Congressman, I was looking at his tie clasp in-stead of his eyes. Your own photographer should be available on such occasions in order to obtain a number of becoming pictures of the candidate with all of the important people present. The pictures for immediate release should be developed and delivered to the Press Secretary for inclusion in press releases about the particular event. Other pictures may be filed and used later in the campaign, possibly with an endorsing statement. *Remember to obtain per-mission from those persons pictured with your candidate before releasing such pictures.*

107

SPEECHWRITER

A candidate will usually develop one or more major speeches which will be repeated during the campaign with slight modifications. A

Speechwriter can add polish, flair, humor, or put an idea or issue into a more acceptable form when necessary. Much of the Research Committee material on issues and opponent weaknesses can be incorporated into the candidate's speeches.

The Speechwriter will also have techniques for rephrasing ideas and issues when speaking to different groups. For example, anecdotes, humor and emphasis used with college students will be different from those used with senior citizens. Local flavor, local interest can be incorporated easily into speech strategy.

The Speechwriter should also be alert to recent facts and information which may be pertinent.

108

PUBLICATIONS WRITER

This is an optional position, but one which can lead to a different kind of media exposure and may result in utilization of the talents of volunteer staff.

During my campaign a woman who was typing as a headquarters volunteer mentioned she was a published author. She offered to suggest some articles about the candidate and the campaign to national women's magazines. We were pleased with her offer and gave consent. As a consequence of this, a national girls' magazine did accept an article about my daughters and how they managed home and father while mother was on the campaign trail. Pictures of the girls cooking and studying were taken by the campaign photographer and were included in the article.

The magazine came out two weeks before the election. The publicity and attention were excellent. Without such an offer from a talented person this good publicity never would have occurred.

In most campaigns talented people surface to add a unique dimension to campaign activities. Campaign staff members should always be alert to the creative capacities of volunteer workers. Too often talented people are left to do trivial tasks, so they drop out of campaign activity because their talents are not utilized in meaningful ways.

109

110

Precinct Organization

Precinct organization represents a vital part of any political campaign. The amount and quality of precinct organization can make the difference between success or failure. A well organized area will yield from 5 to 25% more votes than an unorganized one.

111

A precinct, sometimes called a ward or election district, is the smallest geographical voting unit in the state. It is usually serviced by one polling place on election day and may include anywhere from 150 to thousands of voters. The precinct standards and boundaries are set by state law. In many states a precinct leader is elected at the primary or appointed by party officials. In California, there are no designated precinct leaders.

The main elements of precinct work are:

1. Precinct canvassing, which is a check of

every household to determine party affiliation, candidate choice, and if there are any unregistered voters.

2. Follow-up registration drives; maintaining lists of new voters.

3. Demographic data collecting and analysis of population, including income and education levels, and issues. (See chapter on Research.)

4. Election statistics gathering: past election results, voter turnout, voting trends, fall-off trends, noncommitted votes, percentages.

5. Precinct targeting — selection of prime precincts in which to work.

6. Polling and surveys.

7. Election day get-out-the-vote effort.

112

Here are the items needed in precinct work, and where they may be obtained:

Item
   Where Available

Precinct Maps
   County Board of Elections

Voter lists
   County Board of Elections

Past election results
   County Board of Elections

Demographic data
   U.S. Bureau of the Census; Congressional district data

Election statistics
   State Legislative Caucus; Office of the Secretary of State

Street-by-street lists
Telephone company; local planning dept. or agency

Local Organizations, club lists
Chamber of Commerce; local coordinating councils

Legislative voting records
Congressional Record; State Legislature

PRECINCT COORDINATOR

The duties of the Precinct Coordinator are to:

1. Serve as a member of the Executive Committee, working under the direction of the Campaign Manager.

113

2. Serve as the coordinator of all precinct work. Recruit and supervise the Precinct Committee consisting of the Precinct Chair, Voter Registration Chair, Get-Out-The-Vote Chair, Transportation Chair and Telephone Chair.

3. In close cooperation with Campaign Manager, plan in detail the precinct master plan, including research, precinct targeting, registration and election day drives.

4. In close cooperation with the Research Coordinator, assist in the design, assignment and completion of precinct research.

5. Call and conduct meetings of the Precinct Committee.

6. Advise committee chairpersons and workers of voting regulations and procedures.

7. Coordinate precinct work with other candidates and central committee headquarters.

VOTER REGISTRATION

In most parts of the United States only those people who have registered in advance to vote will be given a ballot on election day. That is why voter registration may be a critical factor in deciding who wins the election.

Registering voters is also a rewarding kind of political action because it brings the registrar in touch with people, enlarges the scope and number of voters, and can mean success or failure to a candidate or party slate.

114

Most communities have voter registration drives which are conducted by both partisan and nonpartisan groups. The League of Women Voters usually conducts a nonpartisan drive in areas where the League is active. Central committee and party candidates spearhead the partisan registration drives.

By law, a registrar may not turn anyone away who wishes to register. Therefore, a partisan voter registration drive concentrates on areas where one's own party's support is strong. Areas where party support is weak are avoided.

The first thing to be done by the Voter Registration Chair is to consult with the County Board of Elections for detailed information about local procedures and regulations. Such regulations will vary from county to county and state to state.

Answers to these questions should be obtained at that time:

Who can register?

What are residency requirements?

Where can people register? List the depots for registration.

When can they register?

What are the closing dates for registration drives?

How can they register by mail?

How many deputy registrars may you recruit for your committee?

Are you allowed a candidate's registration committee?

115

It is up to the Voter Registration Chair to make it convenient for people to register. If the act of registering is made easy, they will do so. On the other hand, if it is inconvenient many will not bother.

Voter registration teams may set up registration tables in the following places: firehouses, schools, supermarket lots, picnics, rallies, parades, county fairs, or wherever numbers of people congregate. Drives also can be conducted at college campuses during school registration. Any high pedestrian traffic area is worthwhile. Obtain prior permission for such operations. Knowledge of and cooperation with the efforts of other committees will pay off in the long run.

Registration drives are usually held in the spring, the drive closing date falling a specified number of days before the primary. Efforts will peak again in the fall, with the closing date a specified number of days before the general election.

Those people who offer to serve as deputy registrars will be so designated by the County Board of Elections, following completion of a workshop course given through the County Clerk's office. The workshops are designed to instruct the new registrar in the procedures and details of registration, to swear them in as deputies, and to sign out the registration books. Payment is made to the deputy registrars about six months after the election and is determined by the number of accepted registrants.

116

Basic registration drive tactics:

From precinct lists, telephone and census lists, determine the names and addresses of persons not registered.

From the same and other sources, determine the areas where high party or candidate support may be found (Precinct Research Team).

Conduct workshops for door-to-door and telephone canvassers.

Conduct door-to-door canvass to pinpoint non-registered voters.

Assign deputy registrars.

Determine locations and hours voter registration tables will be set up.

VOTER REGISTRATION CHAIR

The Voter Registration Chair works directly under the Precinct Coordinator and in close cooperation with the Get-Out-The-Vote Chair and the Precinct Chair.

The duties of the Voter Registration Chair are to:

1. Research local regulations and procedures, and inform campaign staff about them.

2. Determine with Precinct Chair, the strategy, tactics and schedule for voter drives.

3. Recruit deputy registrars.

4. Arrange with County Clerk or County Board of Elections for registration classes.

5. Coordinate with political party structure and other candidate committees for drives throughout the area.

6. Direct the registration drive.

7. Maintain lists of deputy registrars and new voters.

8. Collect completed registration books, return to County Clerk or Board of Elections.

TARGETING THE DISTRICT

In a congressional or state senate district, a quarter of a million people may cast votes. Instead of working precincts indiscriminately, you can determine early in the campaign where your potential votes are. Remember that every voter is not a potential convert to your candidate. Surveys have shown that most communities display

117

the same voting patterns from election to election. Change in voting behavior is predictable. Since you will want to work hard where it will count, and to write off those areas where it won't, it is essential that you find those precincts where your potential is high.

These are the steps in determining which are the priority precincts:

1. Analyze the results of the last two primary and general elections to determine:

Party registration. Over 60% for one party is considered a "safe" district for that party.

Party voting loyalty. Even though a district may have a 55% or more registration in one party, the votes in past elections may show a sizable switchover at the polls.

Drop-off from top office to lesser offices. Do people only vote for president and senator, and then stop?

Past support for ballot issues. How do voters feel about environmental issues, school tax elections?

Vote contribution. Where are the large turnouts, and are they potentially in your camp?

2. Obtain U.S. Census data by tract to show distribution by age, sex, income, ethnic groups and other demographic information. This data can tell you which precinct has a high senior population and which has high-income property owners.

3. Determine where the "swing" or inde-

118

pendent vote is. Uncommitted votes may comprise 20% of the vote. Determine how they affected past campaigns.

This information can assist in planning selective mailings, effective telephone and get-out-the-vote campaigns. You will be able to determine the attitudes of voters in the high priority areas as distinguished from voters in secondary areas.

PRECINCT CHAIR

The Precinct Chair works directly under the Precinct Coordinator, in close cooperation with the Voter Registration Chair, the Get-Out-The-Vote Chair and the Telephone Chair.

The duties of the Precinct Chair are to: **119**

1. Recruit precinct workers.

2. Plan and conduct training workshops for precinct workers.

3. Plan and direct:
   Precinct canvassing,
   Telephone canvassing,
   Precinct literature distribution and
   Precinct walks with candidate and workers.

4. Work closely with Transportation Chair for election day coordination.

5. Prepare the precinct workers kits for canvassing, distribution of leaflets and flyers.

GETTING VOTERS TO THE POLLS

Personal contact represents a most effective way to get people to vote and to influence them to vote for the "right" candidate. The precinct worker is the basic means of contacting the voters and of persuading them to exercise their privilege of voting.

Priorities in precinct work are to find out who the supporters are, to keep them enthusiastic and committed to the candidate, and to discover and convince the uncommitted voter to cast a ballot for the candidate. It is best to ignore those persons you know to be "on the other side." It is important not just to carry the precinct, but to carry it with the greatest number of votes possible. Losing a precinct by the smallest margin or winning it by the largest margin is vital to winning elections.

120

Thorough planning is of utmost importance in precinct work; workers will perform their assignments only as well as they are organized.

Workshops should be planned to give the precinct worker a firm understanding of what the task is and how it should be done. The packet which is prepared for the workers use and directions about how to use it are vital. How to make initial contact with people, what kinds of information to give to voters, what kinds of responses to make to questions are all things the precinct worker should know. Some basic rules for the precinct worker are:

1. Be brief.

2. Be a good listener.

3. Be polite.

4. *Never argue.*

5. Leave on a note of friendliness.

PRECINCT WORKER'S PACKET

The precinct worker packet should include:

1. Precinct map. Clearly define the streets the precinct walker should cover.

2. Precinct list. During a precinct canvass, supply the worker with a precinct list for that area. Precinct lists may be transferred to one 3x5 card for each registered voter on the list before the canvass for convenience in assembling data later.

121

3. Literature for distribution.

This may include any candidate material such as brochures, bumper stickers, door hangers, window signs, etc.

For the primary election, supply precinct lists that have been updated from canvass data, and distribute literature to party members only.

In general election, precincting may include distribution of other-candidate material or slate material.

The packet may also include suggestions for handling voter questions that the precinct workers may have difficulty in answering. It may suggest the best days of the week or the best hours of the day to reach people in their homes.

Precinct workers should be encouraged to return precinct maps, lists, all undistributed materials, and to make evaluations on how they and the candidate materials were received by voters.

GET-OUT-THE-VOTE CHAIR

The Get-Out-The-Vote Chair works directly under the Precinct Coordinator and in close cooperation with the Voter Registration Chair, the Precinct Chair and the Transportation Chair.

The duties of the Get-Out-The-Vote Chair are to:

1. Assist in recruiting precinct workers.

122
2. Plan and direct the activities on election day.

3. Recruit, train, assign poll workers.

Campaign Manager

Selecting a Campaign Manager is the most critical decision a candidate makes. In most political campaign books, the discussion of the Campaign Manager comes at the beginning of the book. This book saves the Campaign Manager's job description until last for some good reasons.

123

If you have read this far, you have a good idea of the scope of campaign activities. If you have been overwhelmed by the vastness of the task, you realize what a Campaign Manager must deal with.

Here is the one person who must be in touch with each component within the organization: understand it, plan it, direct it, coordinate it, correct it, reorganize it, eliminate it, supervise it, delegate it. This is also the person who will be blamed when things do not work or do not work smoothly. The candidate, rather than the Campaign Manager, reaps the rewards of success. In short, it is a complex, difficult and thankless task.

Most campaign manuals are vague about the "lesser" jobs in campaign organization; frequently people who hold those jobs don't see their roles clearly. No one is sure where he or she fits in. Since all jobs discussed in this handbook are vitally important to a successful campaign, the people who fill them are equally important.

Each of the tasks described must be accomplished during the campaign. You cannot omit any of the fundamental components, although you may discard titles or combine functions. For instance, you may eliminate the Precinct Coordinator and combine all precinct activities under one person. You can place telephone and transportation jobs within the scope of the Headquarters Manager. Scheduling and Aides Chairs may merge into one job for one person. You will not, however, be able to eliminate media, precinct operations, financing, personnel coordination, scheduling or research, if you expect the campaign to get off the ground.

The details of your campaign organization will be determined by the particular needs of your district. A congressional campaign will probably need an organization which resembles the full scope found in this handbook. A campaign for state legislative office in an urban area may need more precinct walkers and telephoners and fewer managers, while a similar cam-

124

paign in a large rural area may need to be structured with mini-campaign organizations in every city or town. The specifics of organization will be determined by the Campaign Manager and the coordinators of media, finance, personnel, research and precinct activities. (See Organizational Chart.)

The Campaign Manager is the person the candidate "gives" her campaign to. All major decisions will be made by that person. How staff positions are delegated, how they function and merge within the campaign structure will depend on how the person she selects envisions the process; how he/she utilizes the talent and energy of workers. That person must be able to plan a campaign strategy based on research, must have a time-line schedule for implementation and must use sound techniques in the process.

125

Two members of the staff, at least, should be paid professionals: One is the Press Secretary and the other is the Campaign Manager. If your campaign decides to hire a professional Manager, be prepared to put out a good deal of money. Because few women are given managerial status in a man's campaign, experienced female campaign managers will not be plentiful. When you hire a woman she will, most likely, be gaining her first experience with your campaign. Too often women may not have sufficient confidence to take on a job of such major proportions, while those with ability may not have the time because of family responsibilities. Qualified men may not want to work for a woman.

I solved the problem by having two persons coordinating my campaign, a man and a woman. They were individuals who complemented each other by being opposite kinds of people, preferring opposite kinds of tasks. There were times when each could do a better job because of his/her sex. There are people who do not want to deal with women at higher levels. When we met with those people or groups, the man coordinator took over. On the other hand, the woman coordinator was superior at working in the world of women, which was where we got our strongest support. Furthermore, the man was more effective in dealing with local and state party officials, while the woman was more effective in raising money. Supporters in the community were pleased when they discovered the campaign was not all female, and others were pleased because women were prominent in decision-making positions. The assets of dual-coordination cancelled out the debits.

Just as there should be a balance of men and women in decision-making positions in a man's campaign, the same should be true of a woman's campaign. Select people who will do the best possible job for your particular situation. A superior staff might get a less superior candidate elected. A poor staff can help defeat a superior candidate.

Generally, a Campaign Manager should be someone the candidate can trust and feel comfortable with; who has political experience; is able to raise money; can represent the candidate

126

in critical situations; and can work seven days a week for fifteen hours a day.

Administrative background is desired, as is experience in one or more of the following: public relations, community organization, media, personnel management, statistics, research. Personal traits to look for are intelligence, creativity, flexibility, high energy, ability to be a tough negotiator. This is what the candidate may need and want, but it will be very hard to find someone with even the minimum qualifications.

Once the Campaign Manager is named, the candidate should clearly define the Manager's responsibilities and the areas where she wants the final word. Then, that person should be allowed to do the job. Candidates often have a tendency to get involved in every aspect of the campaign. Not only is that time consuming, but it may impede the work of the Campaign Manager and of the campaign itself.

127

The selected Manager should be given about a month to get into the job. If at the end of that time, the candidate's appraisal of the work done is negative, she should get a new Campaign Manager. This is such a critical position, the candidate should not cling to someone who is not doing the job for whatever reason. If she loses confidence in her Campaign Manager, the morale of the entire campaign can be seriously damaged.

128

Postface

2/79

To those women who will be candidates or key staff members, part of your job will be to serve as models for the women who will follow you. It will take time before significant numbers of qualified women are seen in the state houses and at the national level as legislators, key staff members, or executives.

129

It has been more than fifty years since American women were allowed to vote. Women still have not reached their political maturity, if we measure political maturity by equal participation and representation within the political process. It may not take another fifty years for that to be accomplished, but it will not be tomorrow. Many more women will have to perceive themselves as politicians and be willing to enter the arena before there will be an equal number of men and women decision-makers in government. That is why, at this point, *every* woman who *runs* takes all women a step toward victory. And the triumph lies in . . . *getting her elected!*